Faith, Grief &
Pass the Chocolate Pudding

HEATHER WALLACE
STUART RUBIO

FOREWORD BY
AMY LOGAN

Faith, Grief & Pass the Chocolate Pudding – 1st ed.
Heather Wallace/Stuart Rubio

Cover Design by Staci Sarkowski/articulate-design.com
Interior Design by AlyBlue Media LLC
Published by AlyBlue Media, LLC

ISBN: 978-1-944328-25-2
Library of Congress Control Number: 2016903405
AlyBlue Media, LLC
Ferndale, WA 98248
www.AlyBlueMedia.com

PRINTED IN THE UNITED STATES OF AMERICA

TESTIMONIALS

"HOPE . . . In Faith, Grief & Pass the Chocolate Pudding, Heather Wallace and Stuart Rubio provide a combination of elements not often found in grief memoirs: wry humor, hard questions without tidy answers, and realistic hope. A welcome and unique contribution."
-GREG ADAMS, LCSW, ACSW, FT Grief Counselor and Educator

"LAUGHTER . . . Grab a piece of chocolate, read Heather and Stuart's book, and get ready for tears to flow, laughter to erupt, and memories of deceased loved ones to surface. These ingredients serve as a hope-filled antidote for the unbidden journey of grief. Not only will Heather and Stu become your new best friends, you will rejoice to find yourself renewed."
FRAN SHELTON, D. Min., Faith & Grief Ministries

"MUCH NEEDED . . . Heather Wallace and Stuart Rubio's book "Faith, Grief and Pass the Chocolate Pudding" is not a traditional book on grief. It is a book about life that happens in the midst of grief and all the other stuff that happens along the way. Heather and Stuart provide a much needed perspective on coping with grief from a Gen X perspective. You will laugh and cry and learn how to speak with the next generation in the midst of the very real and confounding experience of grief."
Rev. Dr. Rob Erickson, Pastor, First Presbyterian Church, Jefferson City

"A MESSAGE . . . Finally, a book about grief so real that you actually find yourself laughing out loud when you thought you'd never laugh again. Heather and Stuart so unselfishly share their experiences – both expected and UNexpected - with the loss of her dad and his brother, as a message for all of us that we are not crazy, that everyone grieves on a different time schedule, and that eventually, things really will start to be okay."
Amy Logan, Author of A Girl With A Cape

"EXTRAORDINARY . . . This book is an unconventional, educational, extraordinary, quirky, genuine, authentic, laugh-out-loud look at grief. Heather and Stuart courageously tackle both the dark and humorous experiences associated with the death of a loved one."
Karen Akin, Pastor for Congregational Nurture, Second Presbyterian Church, Little Rock

DEDICATION

To my dad,
John witt Wallace
-HEATHER WALLACE

To my brother,
James Robert Rubio
-STUART RUBIO

CONTENTS

BY AMY LOGAN

FOREWORD

Best book on grief. Ever.

Why? Because it's real. Because it tells you you're not crazy. Because even though you're in the midst of grieving and there's all this noise and confusion in your head screaming at you with the "what ifs," the "I should'ves," and the "*YOU* should'v es," ... This book is the sweet whisper from Heather and Stu saying, "I get you. You're not crazy. It's gonna be okay."

And they do.

And you're not.

And it is.

Spoiler alert – no one makes it out of here alive.

There's a "*Screw you, I'm not coming in to work tomorrow*," thought if I ever heard one. But it's the truth. And it might not seem so bad knowing that death is going to happen to you. To me. To all of us. We "get" that, right? I mean, duh.

But, what we *DON'T* get, and what is so unfair about all of this, is that it happens to those around us, to those we love so intensely, without any warning whatsoever.

Just *BAM*.

Death.

I mean, sometimes there's warning – there's a prolonged illness, there's age, but even then, no matter the cause of loss. . .

WE are left.

Here.

To go on with that unapologetic void.

I lost my sister in 2014 to a long battle with breast cancer. The weeks that followed were almost unbearable because with her death came so much more loss than we ever could have imagined. And I'm telling you, there was a LOT of crazy that apparently still lived inside of me and this was the perfect storm for it to make its grand appearance. Grief can and will take you to the edge just because it feels like it; just because it can.

It was somewhere within the first couple of weeks after my sister died that Heather sent me this book to read. At first she felt like an awful friend, poor thing, and swore up and down that she wouldn't be offended if I didn't want to read it. She sent me mile-long texts (I'm not kidding...MILE-LONG!) explaining herself; making sure that *I* knew that *she* knew she was an insensitive jerk for sending it to me right when she did.

But honestly? I think deep down, she knew it was exactly what I needed – something to focus on, while sitting at home, NOT self-medicating, NOT drowning in cheap wine, NOT sobbing uncontrollably. And certainly NOT beating myself up with the loud, condemning voices in my head even if for only for a few minutes. Sound familiar?

I started reading.

And there was laughter.

And tears.

And more serious laugh-out-loud laughter!

And then there were CHARTS!

Charts that showed me where I fell exactly on the crazy scale! Hold up! They actually have a crazy scale chart? And somebody else is on the same side of the scale as me?! And then there was a feeling of normalcy without being judged. There was this overwhelming feeling of, "You're *not* crazy. Yes, this sucks, but you will get through it. It will hurt, and sometimes *really* badly. And you will make stupid decisions even when you think all the crazy is out of you. BUT! You will get through it."

That was what I needed to hear. It's what we ALL need to hear. Truth. Rawness. Vulnerability that we can take comfort in. Knowing that we are not alone; that we are not all going to follow the DABDA scale of grief and loss at the same time or in the same order (Ahem . . . denial, anger, bargaining, depression, acceptance . . . high school Death & Dying class, 1988). These stages of grief are not universally recognized by all grief counselors anymore. And that's OKAY. It wasn't until I read this book that I realized you don't *have* to get over it. That it might *always* just suck. That time doesn't *always* make it completely better. But at the very least, at the very, *very* least, it will eventually get less awful.

And it does.

Heather makes you feel like she's your long lost friend who returned from traveling the world just in time to help get you through this. She came back for *you*. She's that friend who gives it to you straight. No beating around the bush, and certainly no sugar-coating.

But...that's not the best part. The BEST part is that she shares her stories; her true real-life, I-can't-make-this-sh**-up-straight-from-the-heart stories which actually make you feel a little bit better about yourself because you start to realize, you start to actually *believe* that you're okay; and that it's always great to have a friend who's *juuuuuust* a little bit crazier than you are.

And she is.

And I am lucky that Heather really is my friend.

And now she's yours.

I hope you find comfort in this book and in your life moving forward. May you live, love, and laugh out loud. And may you never get pulled over wearing even your best lingerie. You're in for a good read. Now, pass the chocolate pudding.

Amy Logan
Author of the book series, *A Girl With A Cape*
Founder of the Kindness Gala

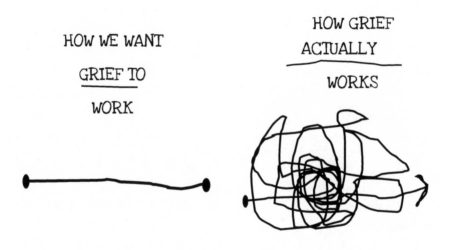

HOW WE WANT

GRIEF TO

WORK

HOW GRIEF
ACTUALLY

WORKS

BY HEATHER WALLACE

PREFACE

Dear Dad,

Okay, I don't actually believe he can read this. But for those who can, I hope this is a book that tells a story about the funny, the not so funny, the sometimes painful and ridiculous places that grief can take you when you lose someone you love. I hope this book tells you that you are not alone in this process. And that you're not crazy. And that insanity, due to grief, doesn't last forever; although I reserve the right not to be held responsible if, in fact, your insanity is not fueled by grief.

If I'm going to talk about the death of my father, however, I'd like every person to at least get a glimpse of Dad's life – how much his life meant to me, how much I loved him, and how I learned to trust people, see the best in them and expect the best out of them, from him.

It is difficult to talk about the aftermath of someone's death without giving equal playing time to their life. I'd like to believe that I represent the best qualities of both of my parents, and what they each taught me about life. I hope that the person I have become conveys that goodness to all who cross my path, today and always.

But just in case Dad is somewhere reading this (I like to cover all my bases): I'm a pretty staunch Christian. People who believe most of the tenants of Christianity have a tendency to hope one's soul goes to heaven after death, and that the soul doesn't hang around here on Earth waiting to see what literary masterpiece one might inspire. Thanks to Dad's conversion to Buddhism just before his death, he believed he would come back as a cricket or a butterfly. Just in case he did (which would be downright irritating to me because I hate to be wrong), and in the off-chance that there's now a cricket or a butterfly lurking about who is exceptionally well-read and likes karate, this book is for you.

When I was a little girl, I always promised Dad I would take my ridiculously huge self-made fortune (which, as it turns out, is the $8.43 balance in my bank account) and build a swimming pool in his backyard. I never quite got there. I happen to know that he believed it was important to have a positive impact on the lives of others, swimming pool or no swimming pool. I hope that this book is my donation toward helping others suffer a little less through their own grief, mostly by using myself as a stellar example of what not to do during the grieving process. Unless you really enjoy rampant humiliation – in which case, follow my lead!

My dad taught all six of his children not to take themselves so seriously, which is something I'd be willing to bet he sometimes regretted. Within this book, I hope there are moments when humor really shines before misery. I miss Dad every day. I hope that I can pass along to my own children Dad's love of reading, movies, music and treating people with respect. I would do *anything* to get one last chance to talk to him.

Dad, this is your virtual swimming pool. I'm pretty sure I had to go off the deep end in order to get you your virtual swimming pool. But either way, congratulations. Or thanks. Or I'm sorry. I'm not sure which.

BY STUART RUBIO

INTRODUCTION

The circumstances that brought Heather and I together as friends are tragic: the deaths of her father and my younger brother. But ultimately, they led us to the same table at a grief luncheon where we learned we could support each other through our individual journeys. And so when Heather asked me to contribute to this book, I immediately jumped at the opportunity. I saw it as a way to not only share a portion of my journey which, like Heather's, has a few amusing elements to it, but it's also a way to share my brother's story and how, simply by the way he lived his life, he taught me to genuinely love and care for others. Jamie was not a perfect person, but he was selfless to a fault throughout his entire short life.

Jamie and I were very different people, yet shared lots of things in common. It's through my immersion in these shared interests that I've been able to keep him close to me since he died. We mainly shared a sometimes unhealthy passion for our favorite sports teams. If you've talked to me for five minutes, I've probably already told you at least once that I'm a Nebraska Cornhuskers fan. Jamie was one of the few people I knew who would stress over the games as much as I do. We could talk for hours about the team, no matter how long it had been since we last talked. My wife will tell you that talking football with another Husker fan usually leaves me frustrated because the other person never takes it seriously enough for me…but it was never that way with Jamie. The Saturday after Jamie died was the first game of the 2014 season. While I will openly admit that I've cried *after* numerous Husker games in my life, this was the first time I cried at the *beginning* of a game.

We also shared a competitive spirit, especially through endurance sports. I always hoped that I could one day convince him to share my love of triathlons. When Jamie was nineteen, he traveled to support me the first time I competed in a half Ironman race. He endured a 104-degree day of sitting around and catching short glimpses of me in the transition area. But in the end, Jamie ran half a mile up a hill so he could run next to me and support me through the last stretch of the race to the finish line. I really struggled that day because I wasn't prepared for the heat, but as soon as I saw Jamie waiting to run alongside me to the finish line, all my pain melted away. This is just a miniscule glimpse of the sacrifices Jamie was willing to make for both those he loved and those he barely knew.

Jamie: You are not only with me when I compete or when I lose my voice over a football game. Your spirit drives me to be a better person. Each and every day.

CHAPTER ONE

YOUR LIFE CAN CHANGE IN ONE MOMENT

Even nearly four years after the loss of Dad, I still cannot bring myself to read any of the devotionals, guides, or books about how sane people cope with grief.

No one tells you that your whole life can change in one moment, and that crazy isn't something that lasts forever. No one should have to feel alone in moments of insanity, sadness and loss. If my pain and my joy can help even *one* other person not feel so alone, it's worth writing about. Grief can sometimes be funny. Not all the time. But sometimes.

In April 2012, my dad passed away. There's nothing funny about that. But, surrounding his death, I became what most regular individuals would consider insane. Not clinically insane. Insane with grief. Insane with loss. Mostly temporarily insane. Insane with grief-stricken humor that not everyone can appreciate.

When Dad passed away that April, people began giving me literature. I work at a church where, when you work for a faith-based organization, people are conditioned to give you pamphlets, books and casseroles during times of grief. I got pamphlets on "what to do if you're grieving." I got enough books to start my own small grief-centered bookstore. With few exceptions, these books are about having faith through grief, grieving through unspeakable losses, and how to cope with your feelings through supportive moments of grace, and relationships with other people. As an aside, one thing I find particularly annoying is that all of these books have pictures of birds, sunsets and lighthouses on the covers. As if grief can somehow be solved or lessened by reading something that validates the long-held belief that it's okay to have unspeakable loss as long as you have some birds on the front cover. I am still seeking the *Idiot's Guide to Grief*, or *Grief for the Everyday Lunatic*. Or, even better, *How To Manage Grief With a Wiffle Bat, Thousands of Jolly Ranchers, Seven Hundred Hershey Bars and a Bottle of Wine*.

Almost four years after the loss of Dad, I still cannot bring myself to read any of the devotional, guides, or books about how sane people cope with grief. From the beginning, what I longed for was a book or pamphlet that doesn't tell me that grief is okay. Grief isn't okay! Nothing about it is okay! I haven't wanted or needed anything that "validates" my feelings. I know my feelings are valid.

From the time I lost Dad, all I needed was for someone to tell me the following. But they didn't, so I'm going to tell you:

- That I'm not crazy, and neither are you. There is still some possibility that I am, I suppose, which may make the reading of this book more enjoyable for some. Or more relatable for those who share my belief that grief can cause some of us to suffer from complete lunacy. If you know me and believe that I am, and always have been, one hundred percent sane in real life, you may not want to continue reading.

- That we can be crazy during certain moments but that this particular version of insanity, tied to grief, doesn't last forever. And that it's okay to be crazy in moments when we're completely grief-stricken.

- That we will get ourselves "back," even if convincing ourselves is the most difficult part. I have had moments of falling apart, but I have ever so slowly pieced myself back together with help.

- That it's okay if grief is funny. So far none of the books featuring birds, lighthouses or sunsets have been funny. Most bereavement-related books are not funny because authors don't want to make light of the feelings others experience while going through the grieving process. However, in my case, a large portion of the grief process has been funny – not just to go through, but also for those who've watched me navigate through it. When I get unnerved, I'm the kind of girl who falls down flights of stairs. And cusses when my dress gets caught (and ripped) in the car door as it's slammed shut while still trying to be cool as a cucumber. None of this is theoretically speaking . . . wait . . . I mean *of course* this book is completely fictional . . .

- That we're not all alone. The worst part of grieving for me has been feeling that I am all alone in the world. The funniest days are those when people break up with you (people, as in your friends) after you've fallen down the stairs, got stuck in an elevator, and got your dress stuck in your car door. Sometimes friends break up with you because they can't handle your "new normal." Grief doesn't exactly give you a "new normal." It gives you a "Please God, don't let me cry in my stupid Cocoa Puffs today" mentality. You have to navigate through it one moment at a time. And you shouldn't have to feel all alone while you're going through it. You should know that someone else has been there, and that most people will love you throughout the journey.

There will always be grief. Unfortunately, that's just a fact. Living and dying seem to go hand in hand. People much wiser than I have suggested that death is just another part of life. Grief is for the living. How we carry it, how we learn to face it, how we find ways to navigate it and how we let it shape our lives is, ultimately, up to each of us. Although, I will admit, it often feels like we're more apt to let grief shape us as it chooses, than to be able to grasp grief and mold it like playdough into something we use to change our lives for the better. I try to always be a good person which, in my case, includes following the tenants of Christianity. As is already evident in this book, however, I sometimes swear. I am imperfect every day, and all too often I miss the mark.

You don't have to believe what I believe. However, I am coming through grief, at the very least, with the following things going for me:

I believe I try hard to listen for God's plan.

I am pretty good at holding hands with those who need me when something goes wrong and, often, just because I feel like it.

I am pretty good at feeding everyone nonstop when someone dies. Laugh all you want, but this is a skill.

I am pretty good at making people laugh, often at the most inopportune moments. I know, I know; it's 50/50 as to whether or not that is a good thing.

I am not, by any stretch of the imagination, a grief expert. I don't know how one earns the title of grief expert, but I am reasonably certain that it is not a course I'd willingly sign up for! But I am a Heather expert, as much as anyone can be. I know myself. I know how and what I feel. I know the depths of heartbreak and loneliness that grief can bring. I know that I am not alone in the emotions that the human condition brings. I am not afraid to share my pain, and the stepping stones I used to gradually return to my relatively small share of sanity.

I set out to write something that would provide some healing and closure for myself. I lost Dad far too soon, without a chance to right my wrongs and, probably more importantly, without an opportunity to say goodbye. Within that lost opportunity, I am slowly re-finding myself. Through writing, I have been given an opportunity to support others in their time of need. Those who are grieving need to know that they are not alone. They need to know they are not crazy. They need to know that someone loves and adores them even when they're lost in the depths of sadness. They need to know that not every day will be the worst day of their lives. They need to know that there is happiness to be found on the other side of sadness, and that there is lucidity on the other side of utter madness. They need to know that there are people who will always stand by their side and love them no matter what.

No matter what, grief cannot steal your memories, or your happiness or your joy. It can temporarily displace them, yes. But grief cannot strip away your goodness. It cannot jerk away the depths of your love for another person. It can make you feel all alone and isolated, even from those closest to you. No matter what, grief cannot steal how much you loved, and continue to love, those you lose or how much they loved you.

Grief can make you cry. It can cause you to do things you thought you weren't capable of. Please read on for some of the most extreme, scathing examples of this type of repulsive behavior.

But no matter what, grief is definitely not the important part of grieving. Remembering is the important part. Remembering the things you loved and appreciated most about someone you lost is the important part. Remembering and loving are the most important parts. You still have memories in your heart that can never be taken away from you. There are a million stages of grieving, no matter what those other self-help books tell you. Healing is a very personal process. Everyone heals at a different speed, and also molds healing differently into their future lives.

I know that my grief is intensely personal. It has different colors and flavors from other people who are mourning the loss of someone they loved. It is my fondest wish that within the chapters of this book you will find something that you might be able to relate to in some small way, which helps you to carry your own grief in a more positive and productive way, and helps you to feel like you are never alone, no matter what. At this very moment, others are grieving just like you. Which means there is always someone you can reach out to. No matter what, you do not have to survive this by yourself. No matter what, there is help available. No matter what, others have been there. No matter what, there are moments even in the depths of grief, that are funny and joyous and ridiculous. I hope you enjoy mine (and Stu's). They are mostly funny and joyous and ridiculous. Actually, mostly ridiculous.

DO OVER:
I make jokes but, in all honesty, I don't actually get a do-over on this round of grief. The best I can have is a "do better" for everyone in my future.

CHAPTER TWO

THE BACKSTORY

Waiver clause: read at your own risk! Actually, please read this part, because you need the backstory.

I am fully aware that many bereavement books feature lighthouses, doves, seagulls, or sunsets on the front covers. You know how those sorts of books offer such nice gestures, and address important, graceful, kind, compassionate moments and techniques on how to survive grief? You know how I've promised you a book that isn't like that? I've promised a book that isn't depressing and full of grief stages, and tells you how to pray or breathe into a paper bag? You know how I've promised a book that doesn't make you want to poke your own eyes out with a fork or a book that doesn't make you wish you hadn't read it because now you *are* depressed and ready to bury yourself in gallons of chocolate ice cream and a *Terms of Endearment* movie marathon? I'm still promising that. Maybe you'll laugh, maybe you won't. But you have to get through the backstory first to understand how all of this started, to understand my own personal brand of crazy.

The backstory is not particularly funny. And now you say "But you promised, you psychotic, narcissistic *jerk*!" I know I promised. I will make it up to you in the rest of the book. But for this chapter

7

get the chocolate, the ice cream and the sad movies ready. My apologies in advance. For the record, my personal pain is not generally something that can be fixed by copious amount of ice cream, if that helps my case at all.

Here's my backstory and how my whole life changed in a moment. For a brief while on April 3, 2012, I was just me. Plain Jane, ordinary forty year-old me. I have never considered myself all that special. I'm one of the masses. Not that special to the entire world, but somehow able to still be special to a few. Weirder than most, but probably also nicer than some. On that particular evening, while our daughter was at choir practice, I was looking forward to an elusive date night with my husband and our youngest son. I happily anticipated visiting our favorite bookstore. I even envisioned our youngest son telling me all about the Greek gods in whatever book he found. I was looking forward to eating pasta at one of our favorite Italian restaurants. And I was ecstatically happy to be out in the nice, sunny spring weather.

It was the kind of day that's nothing to write home about, but calming all the same. I was wearing my favorite new pink sparkly flip-flops. They were a style that was impractical for any occasion, but I bought them anyway. When the sunshine hit my feet, those flip-flops reflected light just like a prism; the glow could light up an entire room. They were an impractical, silly style that generally served no purpose other than to function as casual wear on nights like *that* night. The kind of shoes that make people like me happy for no reason. A pair of shoes for April 3. One pair of sparkly good-for-nothing shoes.

And then, in one moment, the flash of light reflecting off the sparkly shoes was taken.

Taken. Stolen from me. Like a thief in the night.

It's strange how this expression is used to convey the fear we feel when faced with something that has been ripped away so unexpectedly. My whole life changed in an instant. In the moments between Italian food and sparkly shoes, between cloudless days and the calm of spring, came a moment when my happiness was stolen. Ripped away.

In that moment, one of the calmer people I know, my younger sister, called me. Dad had suffered a massive heart attack and was at the hospital. The doctors were trying to fix it. It looked okay. Maybe okay. They were waiting to see him. And did I want to come to the hospital? Her voice was calm, but I knew she was scared. Scared but hopeful.

In God's infinite wisdom, at that very moment we happened to be dining in an Italian restaurant that wasn't far from my sister's house. Within moments, I was by her side, and together we raced to the hospital.

For any human being who has watched medical drama shows, you know that hospital waiting rooms are fairly predictable. Everybody has seen the TV dramas, and you know who the players are: doctors, nurses, interns, the patients, and the silent janitor wandering the hallways pushing a mop and bucket as if this was a zombie apocalypse movie. And – last but not least – the family waiting nervously and anxiously in the wings. The family with anxious and hopeful looks on their faces. Waiting impatiently. And hopefully.

People who don't have brothers or sisters, or who aren't close to them, may find this statement difficult to understand: If you have siblings you are close to, you know their sh#$. You've seen them in the best of times and the worst of times. You've seen them when someone has broken their heart. You've seen them throw up from the flu. You've seen them cry on the pitcher's mound. You've seen them win. You've seen them lose. You've seen their best bikini look. You've seen their worst violin recital. You know their biggest flaws and their biggest triumphs.

And you know when they're faking a smile. You know every look; happy and sad. You know everything in between. And you know their faces. They can't bullsh$% you. Generally.

That day, my youngest sister and I stood in an elevator and, from the moment the elevator doors opened, we could see our younger brother and another sister talking to the doctor. The doctor's back was facing us. So all we could see were the faces of two of the people whom I know best in the world. In that millisecond, I knew hope wasn't going to be enough. I knew from my siblings' faces that it wasn't going to be okay. Not at all.

And, as every worst fear took hold that day, the prognosis got worse. And worse. And worse. There comes a time when you convince yourself that it can't get any worse. You tell yourself it can't possibly get any worse. But, in one of life's cruelest ironies, as it turns out, it can. It can get worse. The thing that every single person in your life conveniently forgets to teach you is that, while the optimists teach us that things can always get better, life can also always get worse!

People sometimes talk about death as a matter of "slipping away." With every fiber of my being, I hope that anyone who reads this book experiences "slipping away" as their only experience with death. Someday when I am feeling either very brave or stupid (or both), I will write a comprehensive chapter about the manner in which Dad passed away. It is still so physically and emotionally painful, I'd rather not write about it just now.

Suffice it to say, Dad was never one to go quietly. There was no going "gently into that good night" for our karate ninja father. He put up an all-out butt-kicking fight worthy of writing about. No, that night he didn't slip away. They resuscitated him to a degree that the doctors later reported as being unheard of. Dad kept coming back, but he couldn't make it all the way back.

Dad talked regularly about getting his butt kicked at the dojo by thirteen year olds, and at karate tournaments by people half his age. He was proud of his karate prowess. He was so pleased that he could get in that karate arena with younger people and withstand the beating; even if he rarely won.

It might just be me making myself feel better but, by the time we saw our dad that final night, his teeth were broken. I like to think he kicked a#$ in there, but finally just had enough of all the emergency room drama and decided to let go. But not without a fight that impressed a whole room of medical staff first.

When I got to the hospital during the early evening hours on April 3, I really thought we'd be there all night. I was ready for a lengthy fight and a sleepless night. I got both, but not in the way I expected. Within an hour or two of our arrival at the hospital, we were informed that everything the medical team had done hadn't worked. Dad's heart attack was too massive, and our father wasn't expected to regain consciousness. In less than a few hours, in a phrase that can't be described but will have to be, for the purpose of this book, as *just like that* – he was gone. He came, he saw, he kicked a#$, and then…just like that, he was gone. Our dad.

Nobody tells you when you still have a chance to make things right with other people that there will never be proper farewells with many of the people you love. For Dad, there was no goodbye. There was no regaining consciousness, no motion picture moment when we stood at his bedside or cried into his shoulder or held his hand and told him all the things we should have said a week ago. My personal goodbye to Dad was two weeks prior to his passing, when I was short tempered, woefully neglectful and impatient with him on the phone as I callously said "I have to call you back, Dad…I have a meeting." And I never called him back. Because I was busy. I was too busy for goodbye.

People say that when someone passes away you will feel angry and hurt and go through denial. It was our choice – my choice – not to continue to resuscitate Dad after they told us that he would be brain dead from the number of times they had unsuccessfully tried to bring him back. It was my choice because, when I reached the hospital that day I was informed that as the eldest child, I was his next of kin. So it was my choice. Something I will sadly and unwillingly live with every moment for the rest of my life. No one tells you that, at some really desperate and ugly point of your life, you're going to say to yourself that you should have made a *different* choice. You should have made a *better* choice. You should have chosen to make the doctors and nurses work for a week straight, if needed, to help him regain consciousness. No one tells you that, inside your own head, you are going to feel like something is screaming while you're trying to remain calm. They don't tell you that even if your heart has been broken tons of times before, that nothing will compare to the pain of your heart cracking in pieces when you lose the man who accidentally started your hair on fire while he was grilling hamburgers. Or who taught you to use a slingshot by making sure he broke every window in the garage. Or who accidentally left the electric sander plugged in just long enough for it to turn on and shave the skin off your arm. Or who taught you that no matter what color, race, religion, sexual orientation or background, everyone deserves to be treated with respect. Or who brought you water in the middle of the night when you cried out. Nobody tells you that nothing will prepare you.

No one - not one person – has the fortitude or courage or wherewithal or foresight to tell you that you will be standing in some Godforsaken hospital staring at your stupid stupid, *stupid* sparkly pink flip-flops wondering how anyone could hate a pair of shoes so much right now.

Nobody tells you that there will come a day when you start out thinking that something, which turns out to be ultimately petty, might seem like your biggest worry. And the very same day might end in your own bedroom on the phone with an organ donation society, answering questions about how your father didn't have mad cow disease, diphtheria, the bubonic plague or any other dreaded disease that might prevent his organs from saving another human being. They don't tell you that everyone will be so nice. So very nice. And that everyone will be sorry. So very sorry for you.

On the night Dad passed, the nurse came in to say for the fifth time that he was very sorry, and asked whether he could do anything for us. In my mind I'm screaming, "YES! Can you get me anything? Liquor! Get me liquor! Right now!" or "Shoes! Give me shoes! I need different shoes right now! *I hate these sparkly flip-flops!*"

But what I really wanted to say was, "Unless you can give Dad back, please, please, *please* for the love of all that is good and holy, get the heck out of my face right now before I say something that I can't take back." Nobody tells you how very nice everyone will be toward you when someone you love passes away. However, for what it's worth, I'd rather have a hundred million people be mean to me if it meant I could have my Dad back. True story.

On the morning of April 4, I was scheduled to be at work. But instead at 7:15 a.m., I was on the phone with a crematorium, an organ donation society, a cemetery, a funeral director, a pastor, a Zen priest, a bagpiper, and everyone else under the sun. And yes, I do know that if you could add a Catholic priest into that mix, it would have most of the same elements as every third bad joke you've ever heard. The voices in my head were still screaming, even twelve hours later. I found myself wondering if the screaming would ever stop. I thought that maybe throwing away the gorgeously beautiful, sparkly flip-flops would help. It didn't. I thought that maybe ridding myself of all of the memories of that day would somehow magically erase the memory of the one thing I couldn't forget – that Dad was now gone. It turns out that you can't make a memory of a loved one go away.

On the afternoon of April 4, I was supposed to be at work. But instead, I was with some of my brothers and sisters trying to pick out a jar for Dad's ashes. A jar. The day after death becomes all about things. Inanimate objects. Because when someone is stolen from you, it is all you can do to think about inanimate objects. You regress to talking about jars and urns, and trying not to talk about the person who is glaringly missing in that moment.

The night Dad died, my baby sister gave me the hospital bag full of Dad's personal effects. We can only assume that when the heart attack became too painful to bear, Dad grabbed his backpack and rode the elevator eight floors down to his apartment complex's management office to ask someone to call an ambulance for him. The lady who worked in the management office was the last person to ever speak to Dad. I wasn't there; yet another fact I'll have to learn to live with. Dad had his backpack with him, so the backpack and everything in it became part of his "personal effects."

At first draft of this chapter, I was lying in my bed, wearing pajamas that I didn't even like. I didn't want to remember hearing the screaming voices in my head while I was wearing my favorite pajamas. I didn't want to risk having to have a pajama burning party like I did with the sparkly flip-flops. As I sat on my bed the next day, I waited for someone to give me direction. Any direction. I found myself surrounded by what was left. *What was left.* Such a stark and lonely statement. I threw all of the contents of Dad's backpack on my bed. Some random vials of Ibuprofen. Two sticks of lip balm. Glasses. A Swiss army knife. There was a package of Kleenex in there, but I used it. At least he left me that much. Two key chains. A handheld game. Two little cases, one with hearing aid batteries. Two books, one about tai chi and one that had my grandfather's name inscribed inside. Dad's cell phone. What was left of his clothes. They still smelled like him. How can they still smell like him if he's not here? His sandals *and* his socks. I can't begin to tell you how many times I lectured him on the finer points of why no one wears sandals with socks. Maybe I shouldn't have wasted all my time and should have traded the "no one wears" for "Forget it, just forget it… I meant to say "I love you." But I didn't.

And a Shotokan karate jacket that Dad was wearing.

No day should end with hugging someone's jacket. No day. It should be an unwritten rule. No grief-stricken jacket hugging. Ever.

In that moment of digging through Dad's personal effects, I realized that I didn't have his hearing aids. I didn't know where they were. How could he have heard what was happening around him without his hearing aids? Did they fall out? Where were they? Why wasn't I there to pick up the hearing aids if they fell out?

I can hear the screaming in my head that's mostly just saying "What kind of God?" right now.

Please don't lecture me about God; if you are a Christian, your God is my God too.

My father had clearly explained the "life isn't fair" lesson to us, from the time we were toddlers. But he left a few things out. He forgot to say that when it's most unfair, you'll be left alone to die with strangers trying to fix your heart. He forgot to say that when it's most unfair, you'll be sitting looking at a pair of sparkly shoes wishing you could trade every good thing you have for one moment of turning back time so you could say goodbye. He forgot to say that you'll miss having your arm grazed by an electric sander. He forgot to say that you would be maybe not all alone, but without *him*, hugging someone's jacket. *His jacket.*

And so my life began again: my life without him. My life with grief. My life with a new version of myself that I had never met before. My life where sparkly shoes would be forever unimportant, and where I would have to realize that love and life and faith might not be as I had expected. My whole life changed in one moment.

DO OVER:

1. Skip the sparkly sandals in favor of more sensible shoes.

2. Don't ever play ball with your dad near a barbecue grill. It could end badly.

3. Always let your dad (and everybody else) wear whatever they want. Socks with sandals, Hawaii themed shirts, favorite raggedy t-shirts, etc. Because in the scheme of things, none of these things will matter in the end.

GRIEF TIMELINES

2 WEEKS AFTER DAD'S DEATH....

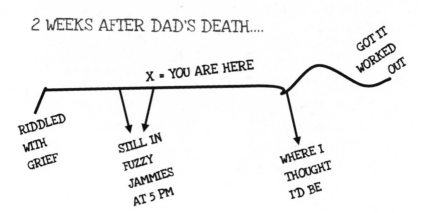

X = YOU ARE HERE

GOT IT WORKED OUT

RIDDLED WITH GRIEF

STILL IN FUZZY JAMMIES AT 5 PM

WHERE I THOUGHT I'D BE

4 WEEKS AFTER HIS DEATH....

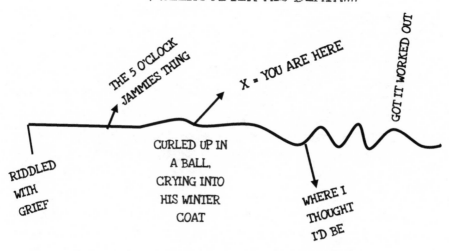

THE 5 O'CLOCK JAMMIES THING

X = YOU ARE HERE

GOT IT WORKED OUT

RIDDLED WITH GRIEF

CURLED UP IN A BALL, CRYING INTO HIS WINTER COAT

WHERE I THOUGHT I'D BE

CHAPTER THREE

LINGERIE

If and when you feel like you're all alone, having some sort of short-lived, grief-filled psychotic break, please read this.

In order to have full disclosure here, you need to know one simple fact about me: I am a prude. This is a plain, simple, unadulterated fact. I am going to give myself the benefit of the doubt and suggest that I may come by this prudishness honestly. I was raised in a place and time when you didn't talk about sexuality. Lest there be too much speculation about this: I may or may not have been raised by wolves. They may or may not have been well-mannered, polite, impeccably groomed wolves. In an attempt to be fair and impartial, I think that there are some good parts to being raised as an impeccably groomed person who doesn't talk about sexuality and feels uncomfortable when things get too highly sexualized. There are things kids these days know that they shouldn't, and sometimes things that adults know that they shouldn't. Forgive me, I may just have inadvertently become my mother. I think sometimes people talk too much. And now, in a moment of unabashed hypocrisy, I'm going to tell you all sorts of things I shouldn't. My mother would be rightfully appalled. My express apologies in advance to my mother who, by the end of this book, will probably tell you that I was, quite obviously, raised by wolves and not at all by her.

In order to understand the abyss that is my version of crazy, you must in some teensy, miniscule way be willing to stretch to some recessed part of the human brain where the terms "appropriate" and "above board" are in some way synonymous with "buttoned up," "dressed like an Amish woman," and "one step above wearing a chastity belt." Confession: Since the first grade, I've been obsessively worried that someone might accidentally see my underwear. So much so that I spent time making sure I always had a shirt to tuck in, that my polos and sweaters were buttoned or zipped to the top, and I usually wore legging and even itchy tights, because they seemed easier to mentally navigate than having to think about what certain horror or plague of Egypt might befall me if anyone *ever* got even the slightest glimpse of my panties or my bra.

Parenting realization here. What, in first grade, is enough to cause a child with this type of mentality an ulcer the size of a small asteroid, makes her among the least complicated children to raise through high school. Are you raising a young girl who's so paranoid that someone might get a glimpse of her underwear that she always wears leggings and buttons her sweaters all the way to the top? If you are, celebrate! I mean it! You are living every parent's dream! There are things you just don't need to worry about that other parents do, indeed, need to worry about. Yes, wolves who raised me, I might have kissed some boys. But I had a complex about anyone ever seeing my underwear. Ever. Friends. Family members. Pediatricians. Makers of underwear. Gynecologists. Dogs. Costumers. Anyone. Problems solved. All problems having to do with sexuality and what the adult wolves called "loose morals" solved.

But things change. And you eventually become a young adult wolf. And, to the great amusement of my best friend in college, I had never worn underwear that was "out of the realm of normal." Quick translation for the non-prudish community: I have never owned underwear that wasn't completely plain. No lace, no nothing. Plain. This goes for *all* kinds of undergarments. And pajamas. My great aunt used to make my sisters and I our own flannel button down pajamas. The very best ones were even embroidered with our names. I cannot tell a lie: these will go down in history as some of my all-time favorite pajamas and, given the chance, if I still had the pink ones with my name embroidered on them and they still fit, I'd probably still wear them.

But with the onset of college came the adventure of a lifetime: the quest to find the perfect lingerie. It seems that only someone who grew up never being allowed to go to the mall with friends could even begin to consider lingerie shopping the "adventure of a lifetime." The wolves who raised me were convinced that only kids who drank, smoked pot, "did the LSD" and got pregnant at age eleven were the ones who would congregate around the payphone at the mall. My apologies to the 99.9 percent of the population who are reading this who actually just went to the mall to drink Orange Julius, or who were there to look at clothes or play at the arcade. Ditto for those who were allowed to go to the carnivals at the local K-mart and also allowed to attend rock concerts. Including the Genesis concert. Certainly I could have fictionalized that group name a little better and gone with 'NSync so you'd think I was a gorgeous twenty-six year old author. Sadly, the wolves raised me never to tell lies. According to the wolves, everyone who's anyone knows that Phil Collins is probably an LSD fiend. My apologies, Phil. "We've got a groovy kind of love," no matter what anyone says. The wolves found stories of "just your typical high school kids not getting into any shenanigans at the mall" less than believable in the real, scary world in which we lived. In college, for the first time in my life, I found myself wolf pack-less, at the mall, and fancy free! *Lingerie shopping!* The wolves were *wrong!* Sexy pajamas weren't just for those in Victoria Secret and Harley catalogs!

My best friend in college went shopping with me the day I bought my very first lingerie. It was actually a silk tank top with matching silk Daisy Dukes shorts adorned with Valentine hearts all over them. Give a girl a break. Did I neglect to mention that was the first lingerie I ever owned? To graduate to shorts and a tank top from the previously buttoned up and "suitable for Mother Teresa" slumber party garb, it was a pretty darn big deal! The biggest! And because life always takes the things you feel you missed out on and brings those back, magnified by one thousand, to haunt and torment you later in life, lingerie became a staple of the soccer mom wardrobe: useful in all situations. Almost.

Confession: I'm never going to be on the cover of any magazine unless eventually running my husband over with my car for his ill-timed desires regarding playing his harmonica inside of our car makes the cut. My husband likes to play the harmonica in the car to aggravate me. Everyone has a fatal weakness. This is his. Breaking his harmonica and throwing it out the car window might eventually be mine. I'm no model. I'm less of a natural beauty and more of a wigged out soccer mom. I'm way more "sweatpants, pigtails and saddle shoes" than "sexy vixen." But I decided somewhere down the road of only seeing myself as plain maybe I didn't have to blend in if I found the right thing to wear. And, well, lingerie is sometimes the right thing to wear. If only just for yourself. Sorry Mom.

But, just like the underwear complex, I would never ever, ever, ever wear it anywhere where anyone might see me, with the obvious exception of the one guy who's seen me in practically every situation and had the misfortune to think he wanted to be committed to me anyway. Most days recently, I'm sure he'd just like to be committing me to some sort of a treatment facility. And no one would blame him in the slightest.

One backstory, so you know exactly what you're dealing with. When our oldest son was born, the night I went into labor was the first opportunity that I had to think clearly and at length about the fact that this guy that I was pretty newly married to was going to see my underwear. I'm not always as forward thinking as I'd like you to believe, quite clearly. I spent the first four hours of the next twenty-some hours in labor having a meltdown over the looming prospect that he was going to see my underwear. Because, let's face facts, when one is in labor, the status of the viewing of one's underwear should be a paramount stressor. You're about to pop a human the size of a watermelon out of a body part the size of a quarter, and your biggest fear really should be the finer points of undergarments. It makes perfect sense. Said no one ever.

One hundred percent lunatic moment. After fifteen hours of intense labor contractions with no drugs, I was completely over the fact that anyone was going to see my underwear or anything else. In fact, at that point, I would not have even cared if someone blasted me out of a cannon; I'm not sure I could even have felt that over the contractions. And at that point, I was willing to try anything. Note to self and others: I am a fan of drugs. Always take the drugs while in childbirth, friends. If only so you can continue to clearly think and worry about the fact that someone might see your underwear. Life is all about having one's priorities straight.

Positive lunatic moment numero dos: If you *also* decide it would be a wonderful, thoughtful, forward thinking, relationship building idea to throw up on the guy you're newly married to, during labor (or any other time), buy lots of lingerie. You're going to need it, because you're going to need something to make you feel like anyone could ever like or find you desirable again. Before labor and delivery, I might have been able to convince myself that I was gearing up to win some award as classy trophy wife of the year. At some point in the labor and delivery process, however, I had this sad epiphany that I officially just threw up on the cutest boy I know, followed by a twenty-seven and a half minute crying jag, followed by uncontrollable teeth chattering, followed by some creative thinking on my part where I tried to back out of the whole "baby having thing" or at least tried to renegotiate my contract to include mind-altering drugs. And he saw my underwear and everything else. At that point, the limited control I had left of my mind made me fully aware that there are times I will not have control of my body. I had a glimmer of hope that maybe, just maybe, the sexiest lingerie in the world might have the ability to dazzle someone (him) enough to make someone (him) forget that he smelled like vomit for a whole day, thanks to me. The depths of memories I prefer no one could recall that are reached in labor and delivery rooms everywhere can only be remedied by lingerie, liquor and intense electroshock therapy, I'm quite sure.

In any case, all of the seemingly important, useless, selectively inane moments of thinking about anyone accidentally seeing my lingerie or my underwear led up to one pivotal, life-changing moment for me. One moment brought on by intense, crazy, psychotic grief.

About a week after Dad passed away, on a bright sunny afternoon I was driving my car when I was stopped by a police officer for driving seven miles per hour over the speed limit. I didn't think they stopped you if you were going less than ten over the limit; color *me* surprised. Maybe he stopped me because I was driving over the speed limit. Maybe he stopped me because I was sobbing hysterically, and my car radio was blaring sad love songs. Nothing says "pull my car over and give me a huge ticket" quite like a soccer mom who is speeding, crying like a banshee, and blaring the greatest hits of Billy Ocean. For most police officers, what would be considered a "routine traffic stop" will be forever remembered (at least by me) as anything but routine.

But, on that fateful day in April, I was blazing down a major thoroughfare in the suburb where I raise my children when I was pulled over by the police. In broad daylight, clad solely in my lingerie, my robe, and my pink fuzzy slippers. My lingerie. My lingerie! Not my pajamas. *My lingerie!!* Here's a picture. Just this. This thing here. And panties. And a robe. All with bows. *Bows!*

I know we live in the times of Fifty Shades of Gray and other fine moments of sexy literature worthy of book burnings everywhere. I know rampant lingerie-clad soccer moms are out there, swirling somewhere else in the universe. I know there are worse things than wearing your lingerie out in public. Off hand, I can't think of anything, but I'm sure there are. There are sexier scandals.

But not in my world. Not at all.

In my world, underwear is something to be respected and feared. Someone might see it! My husband might see it while I was giving birth to his child! Someone might know I wear it! Someone might think something of me based on what underwear I was wearing. Oh sweet mother of pearl the hours I had previously spent thinking of ways to ensure that no one ever saw my underwear! The horror! The tragedy of it all! The modesty police might get me! I'd be on the Jerry Springer Show if someone saw it! I'd make the daily headlines! There'd most certainly be some special circle of hell reserved solely for me! GOD would know! I don't claim to know everything about God, but if I had to hazard a guess, God loves me, but must frown on those who joyride in their unmentionables, right?

And just like that, I got pulled over by a young, unsuspecting police officer. Little did he know what he was in for. Not many men can handle the force of nature that is a soccer mom who just lost her dad, and is driving like Cruella Deville clad only in lingerie and matching panties. Under these circumstances, especially with Billy Ocean's "Suddenly" blaring in the background, any man with the courage to pull me over not only has my undivided attention, but also my utmost respect. He's a brave man. Or a crazy man. Not sure which. Mad props to him. And then the moment the young police officer reached my driver's side window, the tears resumed. Mine, not his. Not just the tears, but the all-out body and gut-wrenching baby sighs, and no holds barred sobbing. I couldn't talk for about twenty seconds. He asked if I was okay. He asked if I had been drinking. I told him I almost never drink. Under the circumstances, I'm not sure he was convinced. All I managed to blurt out was "My dad died a few days ago. *Oh my God.*" Lord's name in vain, apologies to the wolves who raised me and all of my former Sunday school teachers. "*I'm wearing my lingerie!*" Sob-sob-sobbity-sob-uncontrollable gasp-long baby sigh-sobbity-sob. "Do....you...want ...my...license.......??" Sob, cover whole face, fix robe. "*Oh my God, I'm wearing my lingerie. Can you see what I'm wearing?* Just *look* at what I'm wearing! Can you *see this?*" It might just have been my imagination, but I'm pretty sure he could see what I was wearing, and I think he was amused in a "great, this might not end as a traffic stop, it might end with someone in the drunk tank" kind of way.

At this point, even with what I'll call "crazy grief brain", I am struck by a couple of fairly lucid, rational thoughts in no particular order: He's going to take me to the police station. Everyone there is going to see my panties. Please don't let anyone see my panties!

Holy guacamole. My husband is going to have to come to the police station and bail me out of jail, where I certainly will be housed with hardened criminals, one of whom will certainly see my underwear. Panties and hardened criminals are not words that belong in the same sentence. I do not want to end up as a ripped from the headlines Grief & Panties episode of *Law and Order SVU.*

Holy rusted metal, Batman. My husband is going to be so aggravated if our insurance goes up because of a lingerie-related ticket. What exactly is the fine for a panty joyriding violation?

Holy schnikes. My husband is going to have me committed for sure when I get home. Maybe I have time to change out of this getup before he takes me to the funny farm.

This police officer knew he had met his match, apparently.

Maybe because I kept talking about my underwear, which got increasingly more awkward as the minutes ticked by. I think he knew that if he asked me to get out of the car and walk in a straight line, he would have to take me to the police station. And everyone should already know that panties and handcuffs are a terrible combination. If you just laughed, please punch yourself in the gut from me. Because I am not that kind of girl.

EXTRAORDINARILY AMUSED YOUNG POLICE OFFICER: *"Honey."* When someone who looks like they're no more than twenty-three years old calls you honey, you know you're in a pathetic state of affairs. *"Honey, I can see you're upset. Do you live around here?"*

CRAZY HOUSEWIFE WHO CLEARLY NEEDS AN EXORCISM OR A BOTTLE OF TEQUILA: *"I live two blocks away. I'm so sorry. Dad died. Dad died. I'm wearing my lingerie. Oh my gosh. You can see my lingerie!"* Stating the obvious is one of my more fabulous grieving talents.

To this day, I'm still hoping that this policeman was married, or dating, or had some previous working knowledge or familiarity with the state of female undergarments, lest I inadvertently gave him some sort of a seedy Mrs. Robinson moment of education.

POLICE OFFICER: *"Honey."* He called me honey again. *"Honey, I'm letting you off with a warning. But I'm going to drive behind you to your house. And you need to go directly home."*

I stopped crying. The sobbing stopped just as quickly as it had started. Clearly my psychotic break decided, independent of the rest of me, that I had one rapidly dwindling window of opportunity. Maybe my panties wouldn't be seen by hardened criminals or the station's fingerprint tech after all.

I drove home.

The young policeman drove behind me.

I think it was so he could write down my address so he could be the first one to respond should there be any kind of domestic disturbance call in the future. I think he knew good drama when he saw it. I also think he thought that the video moments made possible by someone in my obviously fragile mental state could serve some useful purpose if he ever wanted to audition for *Cops*.

And so that day, I became the Lady Macbeth of suburban American. Overly dramatic, sobbing, major bedhead, clad in lingerie. "Out damned spot." -Shakespeare

As the young policeman pulled out of my driveway, seemingly satisfied that I actually lived there or, at the very least had the garage door opener for that particular house (it helped that the garage door actually raised when I pressed the button) I sat in my car in my garage, finally slightly lucid and letting the grief sink in. When I calmed down, I was left with the following questions for myself, most of which are still unanswered to this day:

How did I get into my car? I have no memory of getting behind the wheel of that motor vehicle.

Where was I going and, even more importantly, did I intend to get out of the car? Because if I did, someone would surely have seen my underwear. No question. There would have been a major panty show going on. And not in a good way. Let's face it, I'm not that kind of a show.

If I had not been pulled over, would I have ended up on the Channel 7 news as a cautionary tale as I wandered through the brussels sprouts at the local grocery store before the police came to take me away? Would I have seen someone I know? Normally, even if I go to the grocery store without *makeup* on, I see twenty-four people I know. That's how karma works in suburban America. So certainly I would have made the New Business or Risky Business section of the school's PTA notes.

Did I believe I had gotten properly dressed that day? This remains perhaps the scariest question because I can only believe that, in my heart of hearts, I thought I was appropriately dressed for going out in public. So if it happened once, could it happen again? Do I need to position a full-length mirror in my garage in case my psyche decides to wander out of my body at some time in the future? Do I need to start keeping a poncho in my car in case my psyche attempts to get even more naked in the future?

A note about grief: It chews you up. Slowly. It eats away at you from the inside. You still look okay on the outside when you're wearing clothing, so it's hard to imagine what is happening to your insides. Your insides start to think that watching week-long Bridezilla marathons and wearing your lingerie in broad daylight to cruise the part of town where your teenage children go to school is okay. It tricks your brain. It readjusts your old normal. It presents you with a new normal. Sometimes a scary normal.

It took me a long time to tell my husband the sordid details of that day. He wasn't home when I received the police escort to our garage. In that moment, I was very afraid that I possibly had turned some corner there might be no coming back from. But I learned something. You can come back. You can decide that what doesn't kill you isn't going to kill you. <u>It might not make you stronger</u>. It might just make you different. Different than you were before. In the days following the event now known as the "Panty Joyriding Police Escapade," I decided that this particular event needed to be the deepest abyss of where my crazy was allowed go. And no deeper. At some point, you have to cut off your own crazy, in case it starts to have a mind of its own and decides to spread like wildfire or a hydra. Having a lifelong fear about someone seeing your underwear is bad enough. Somewhere along the road, probably long before I ever contemplated having a baby, I should have learned that having someone inadvertently, or purposefully, see my underwear was *not* the worst thing in the world. Maybe only the second or third worst thing. I also should not have had the kind of hour-long psychotic break after Dad's death that forced me into a situation where I'd have to confront my fear and my grief simultaneously. It has been, and is still, a long way back. But since that day, I've tried to be really honest with myself about the things I'm truly afraid of, and deal with them head on instead of letting my worst fears confront me in parking lots or on the side of the road. I think I will end up better because something split, twisted, and broke inside me that day. I'm not completely sure I can say the same for that poor police officer.

I have included one picture of what I was wearing that day, so you'll have some perspective. For those who thought my lingerie would look more like the cover of *Maxim* magazine, I'm not sure if "Good for you," or "Shame on you," or "Thanks for not thinking I was a schoolmarm persona," applies here. It certainly wasn't garters or anything that would make the cover of either the Victoria's Secret catalog or a biker girl magazine. But for me, and for grief, "We've come a long way, baby." And not necessarily all in a good way.

For those who thought I'd be wearing something like this, thank you for refusing to believe I still wear ponytails and sweatpants to bed. Even though I do. And shame on you for picturing a soccer mom in a getup like this. And if you wish this lace up leather thing was what I was wearing because it would make the story better, I'll add you to the list. My husband is probably on that list too.

DO OVER:
#$%&???? I have no idea how I could have done this day any better.......always keep a sweater in your car? Or a trench coat?

CHAPTER FOUR

THE FIRST LETTER

If and when you regress to writing letters to people who are no longer in your life, or yelling at them, read this.

I woke up one morning, and I thought I was crazy. Okay, so that may or may not have been the first time that has happened. All I wanted was to say a few pertinent things, not to an audience, but to him. To Dad. Here is my first letter to Dad, post-mortem.

Dear Dad,

I think there are things in life that are supposed to make sense, aren't there? Because they really don't. Why don't they tell you that in the life manual? I don't know how things can make sense when you feel like you're living a nightmare that you didn't sign on for. I still have those days when I lie in bed in that still, small, quiet moment when you first wake up, before my brain is all the way awake, when I forget how my life has been altered. I forget. Sometimes I have that tiny moment of waking up peacefully, which is truly only coupled with huge guilt when I fully wake up and remember what's real. I still have about ten seconds, before I'm all the way awake, where I have forgotten that you're not here anymore. And it's a nice ten seconds. Sometimes nicer than the entire rest of the day.

I know that you would want me to be happy. I know that you would tell me that only sissies cry. As an aside, I would like to point out that if you do want me to be happy, you might consider changing the word "sissies" to "vulnerable individuals." That just makes it sound so much nicer, don't you agree? I can't even begin to admit what a sissy you'd think I was if I truly thought you could see everything that had happened to me over the last few months. I don't think you'd be proud of who I've become, or who I'm becoming. I think you would have liked the old me better. I definitely liked the old me better. What happened to the happy-go-lucky version of me?

It is difficult to be happy-go-lucky when you are grieving. Who knew? There should really be a manual for this stuff. Maybe this *is* that manual.

This week it will be six months. Six months since you left us. Left me. Left me to my own devices. Who thought that was a good plan? Not me, that's for sure.

I can only speak for myself when I say that there's a certain irony that goes with not actually having someone to straighten you out in the time that you most need to be straightened out. There are really only a handful of people who are allowed to straighten me out. It's just the way life works, whether any of us want to admit it or not – only a select handful of people have earned the right in any of our lives to be listened to in moments of intense life straightening out. There are only a few people who have earned the privilege (I'm not at all certain they consider it a privilege) to "speak into" my life in the most difficult moments. The phone might ring, but there are really only three phone calls that have the potential to change the balance of power in my life, as far as I'm concerned. Dear Dad: Where the heck are you when I need someone to straighten me out? I just don't think I can do it for myself right now. I don't know how. I've forgotten how. I can't remember who I was before April. I can't find that girl. I don't know where she is. She's gone. I can't seem to find her anywhere. I just can't do it.

*There is a quiet desperation for me in knowing that, in the midst of heartbreak and chaos, I got a new job that is already changing my life. Somewhere where my faith will be tested every day, for better or worse. This weekend I held a candle in my hand and my hands just shook and shook as I talked to this huge group of kids about faith and blessings in our lives. Because I usually really believe all of that with my whole heart, but right now I'm super angry at God (and at you) and I kind of think it's crap. This week, I just don't know. This week I feel like there are a select few things I've asked God for and, while fairness is promised to no one, I'd like to think that something will work out right. I'd like to think there's hope for me yet. Or still. Or just that there's **hope**. Anywhere. That the events of the last few months won't be the standard for the rest of my life.*

I can hear the whispers. The whispers from my friends. Sometimes I can see it in their eyes. There are a few of my very closest friends who know where I stand, and who know that the battle I'm fighting is with the only person I can't get rid of...myself. I am a powerful arch-nemesis, for myself. I am my own worst enemy. I know my friends don't know how to help me. I know they get tired of hearing about grief; every person can only be tolerant of the struggle of others up to a certain point. People want to go on with their lives. They love me, but they need to return to life-as-usual. And yet, in my head, it's as if time continues to stand still. The battle rages on. The battle is about faith and love and joy and happiness. The battle is about what's real, what's only in my crazy, grief-stricken brain and where the pieces of what's left of me all will fit together through the healing process. The battle rages all around me and I feel like I'm watching someone else's story, like in a movie.

Please tell me how to make sense of something that doesn't make any sense. Please tell me how to stop wanting to just yell out in the middle of the night until you bring me a glass of water, like you always did when I was a little girl. Please tell me how to stop wondering or feeling guilty or regretful because I didn't call you immediately back after the last time we talked on the phone. Please tell me how to stop having regret for every time I complained about having to hear your stories about either stupid karate or the stupid dojo. Please just come back and I promise I'll listen to every story about wonderful karate and the wonderful dojo. See, I've already changed my attitude, I pinky swear.

I'm not wearing my pink sweatpants anymore. Did I neglect to mention that I wore pink sweatpants for almost three weeks straight after you died? Because I did. Until Dave (my husband) told me he refused to go out in public with me if I didn't agree to change. That day I'm pretty sure I wore blue sweatpants, as a sign of rebellion, none of which makes any sense to any rational human. I stopped wearing the pink sweatpants, and I graduated to slowly getting back to "life as I know it." All of these letters and stories; I'm saving them. I'm writing them into a book because someday someone else will think they are certifiably crazy while grieving the loss of their loved one, and I want to be able to hand them a book that's only marginally sad, but also shows the depth of crazy, and be able to say;" I've been there." I want to be able to say to someone else who is grieving: "You are not alone. You are not psychotic. You can wear whatever you want. For the love of Pete, wear the pink sweatpants! You will be okay. People will still love you. People will understand." I guess that's where I am today. I am so sad and so regretful, and there's nothing I can do about it. Nothing. Not-a-single-thing. Things seem so complicated right now, and all I want is for you to call me to tell me to change the oil in my car, just like you always did. Or send me a stupid card with a monkey on it, just like you always did. Or lecture me on how I should always keep gloves and a hat and a window scraper in my car "just in case." Or make sure that I don't let my gas tank get below half a tank so I don't run out of gas on the highway.

I cannot handle how memories of you seem to be everywhere, which is something that is visible every single day. You are in every conversation, in every butterfly that crosses my path, and in every third vocab word that people use in front of me. Everything reminds me of you. I can only blame the same kind of misfortune which happens when you hear a song you can't handle on the radio, or when something reminds you over and over of how much you miss someone. I miss you one billion butterfly wingspans wide. You believed that you'd "come back" as a butterfly or a cricket: it seems that I am now followed by creatures of both species; almost in an Alfred Hitchcock-esque way (refer to The Birds).

The guy I married is building an office in our garage. Needless to say, there is an electric sander in our garage. The second he ran it and I smelled the sawdust, I couldn't stop crying. Every sander and power tool triggers a memory of you freaking out when you accidentally left the electric sander on and it flew off your sawhorse and singed my nine year old skin.

I am still angry. And not about the electric sander. I don't know if I believe that people have a "time to die" or not, although that is one view that has been offered to me over the last few months by more than one person. This view and other views of "why death happens" have been offered as peace offerings, from a variety of sources, because some members of the general public believe I shouldn't continually blame myself for your untimely demise. I think maybe people don't understand that – no matter what the sentiment – no view or helpful, well-meaning piece of advice will take away the blame I place on myself. No view can ever change the last few moments of your life. No belief, no faith and no God can save me from what I believe I should have done. And – just like these things work in people's lives – forgiveness of self is something that many teach, but far fewer are actually able to practice. But it doesn't matter, I guess. Because – no matter what I believe, you're not here anymore. And I will never know. I will never know what I should have done. What I might have said. Who or where I might have been if my whole life didn't take a terrible turn on that sunny day in April.

Who, in their right mind, is in physical pain, especially chest pain, and tells people he's feeling horrible and his chest hurts, but doesn't consider going to the doctor until late afternoon? Why didn't you go earlier, when you should have? Why didn't you call? You called to remind me to change the stupid oil in my car every three months. What could you have been doing that was so important that you didn't go to the hospital? Why didn't you call?

Why didn't I call you?

Why didn't I?

Why?

I am now left with questions. Lots and lots of unanswered questions. Ones that can never be answered to my satisfaction. Ever.

Is there ever peace to be found in the soul of a person who loses themselves in the valley of the shadow of death? How do you remember who you were, who you are, and who you're trying to be? How do I get that girl back? The girl who was happy and joyful and had it mostly together? Okay, mostly might be stretching it. But just a little.

How do I find her and will I still recognize her if I <u>do</u> find her? Is this new reality my forever reality? I miss you.

Love,

Heather

CHAPTER FIVE

ELECTRONICS AND PARKING LOTS

A Short Note on Grief

Lots of people say grief will get better. People who have been there will tell you it's not going to get better, but it will get less awful. In my case, I've just spent the better part of the last forty-eight months counting on the fact that "less awful" actually translates to "less likely to dissolve into an ugly puddle of hiccups and tears in the bathroom, in the sanctuary of church during worship, in the Pepsi aisle at the grocery store, or in the middle of Best Buy." Grief. It gets less awful.

Dear Best Buy Customers:

*I absolutely promise you, nobody but **nobody** feels that strongly about electronics. If someone has a public crying episode which includes heavy weeping and gnashing of teeth on their sales floor or in their parking lot, it's not about the status of a digital camera or high definition television. Please be kind and please visit the store again. All is right with the world of Best Buy. I promise.*

Love,

Heather

DO OVER:

Be gentle to your psyche when you are grieving. I'm sure there are millions, err.....thousands....err.....lots.... err....at least two other people who have cried at Best Buy. If it's still making you cry five years into the grieving process, you may want to consider either waterproof mascara, or shopping elsewhere.

CHAPTER SIX

SPEAK SOFTLY & CARRY A LASAGNA

If and when you don't know what to say or do when
someone you love experiences the loss of a loved one,
read this.

I begin with Buddhism. An Eastern religion that I cannot even begin to pretend to understand. Maybe because I never studied enough. All colleges, universities and higher learning institutions should really have twelve libraries and one bar, not the other way around, if you ask me. Dad would have told me that I should have studied more. I have to cut myself a little slack here: I have been some semblance of Protestant for my entire life. Except for one day when I decided to be agnostic. Anyone who has been to college knows what I mean. Deciding you're not sure what you believe is important, at least for one day. It's very "hipster." Especially when you decide to pair being agnostic with argyle socks.

A few years before Dad died, he became a Buddhist. He was born Presbyterian. As an adult, he attended United Church of Christ until he became a full-fledged Buddhist a year or two before he died. He used to say that the more he read about Christianity, the less he could believe that what they said was true. Which I guess in some way is ironic, because if you raise your children to be good

Protestants, and at least *one* of them goes on to work at a church, and then you completely run away from your Christian beliefs like the black plague, it makes for some very interesting Christmas and Easter dinner conversations. For about a year before his death, he had been regularly attending a Buddhist temple, taking classes and studying about Buddhism. He talked about things like "continued consciousness" and people who believed they would reincarnate as a cricket or a butterfly.

This isn't breaking news. Many American Christians think that the world revolves around only Christianity. They don't understand Buddhism any better than I do. But for many Christians, you're either a Christian or nothing. And so, shortly after Dad suffered a massive heart attack and subsequently decided he'd had enough CPR, the "gift of speaking Christianese" began. Can you tell I'm still aggravated at him? Because I am.

It began because, frankly, I have worked for a church for practically my entire adult life. And good church people often need a place to use their (sometimes) polite church lingo.

People so desperately want to say the right thing when someone dies. They want to be able to comfort you in your time of sorrow. They want to ease your pain.

What I wish I had known before Dad passed away, that I know now is simply this: there really aren't any right words. The people who said what I needed to hear were either people who had "been there" in their own lives, or people who just said they were so sorry. But there are truly no right words. I have one very close friend who has been there, and he sent me a private message with one piece of advice. He told me to try to remember that people mean well. He warned me that at some point people will say things with good intention but, instead, it would actually make me want to pick up an ax and kill them. He told me not to kill anyone, because people mean well, but they just don't know what to say. His version of that piece of advice saved my life more than once. And it also saved the people who I wanted to kill with an ax. Because, of course, he was right. Well-meaning people are sometimes the dumbest, most hurtful people of all. But they *do* mean well.

You know what's the worst of all? The people who don't say anything. Like it never happened. The people who run away or stay away from you for fear of the awkward silence that comes when they don't know the right thing to say.

While there aren't any correct and perfectly healing words, the most painful experience for someone who is grieving is to be anywhere where others pretend the loss didn't happen. Or when you feel like a pariah because people avoid you because your loved one just died. I certainly didn't want to talk about my Dad's death. I still don't. But I can't pretend it didn't happen, either. Because it happened. It happened to me. It's the first thing on my mind, even when it's the last thing on yours. So please don't say nothing at all or avoid me like the plague. Having people say the wrong thing felt like knives next to my skin. Having them say nothing at all felt like razor blades cutting *into* my skin.

Because Dad passed away close to Easter Sunday, it wasn't more than a day or two before people began to use the gift of "Christianese" on me. Again, in case you missed this part, I have almost always worked on a church staff. I can flip any phrase that well-meaning Christians use when someone dies, and make most of them funny. See my chart after this chapter. People will say, "It was God's will." They will say, "God must have needed another angel." They will say, "It is part of God's perfect plan." They will say, "Your loved one is in a better place." My all-time personal favorite is "With the crucifixion and resurrection of our Lord and Savior Jesus Christ, you must be *so* happy that your dad is in a better place." Forgive the sarcasm.

Let's analyze the previous sentence. Yes, it's true, I do work at a church, which leads an individual to some notion that I care about your Biblical knowledge and that your academia is always duly noted. But I still don't care if you are biblically aware enough to turn a phrase about crucifixion or resurrection and relate it back to the passing of my dad. It doesn't impress me. When it comes to grief, I'm just like any other human being. Maybe a little more like a seven-year-old human in this case. When people say "He's with our Lord," or "Thank goodness he's in a better place," or another favorite "He is dancing with the angels in heaven," it doesn't make me feel better. At least if they had managed, in honor of Dad, to spin it like he was doing karate with the angels in heaven, I might have thought it was a little funny. But the truth is, Dad was a Buddhist. So for word-nerds like me, saying something about coming back as a cricket or a butterfly or chanting or transcending time and place might have impressed me far more.

The lowest moment of that week, other than his death, was someone who said that it was "Too bad (your) Dad had become a Buddhist, because he wasn't saved and we wouldn't be seeing him in heaven." I could probably write a whole book about things that people should never say, not just related to death and dying. I still don't know where I'd put this particular phrase, except in a category that I like to call "things I have no idea where to put in my brain which have lessened my faith in humanity." If you've ever been punched full-out in the gut, and I have because I have five siblings, that's the feeling you get when someone says something like that to you.

Prepare to be offended by my less than appropriate language. About halfway through the week after Dad died, someone came to the door and asked what my family and I needed to help us "get through the week." They asked if we "wanted anything." When they walked away from the door, the Inigo Montoya (Princess Bride reference) in me said, "I want my father back, you son of a b#$%^." Right out loud. Luckily my husband was standing right there, in a good place to appreciate my humor. And he generally loves me and watches the very same movies that I do. What do I want? What *do* I want? The answer to the question is pretty simple, although multi-faceted. I want my father back. Give him back to me. Not in a box of ashes. And if you can't give me what I want, then please quit asking what I want. I have some other things I want, but they are going to come out in some chapters elsewhere in this book, and they are likely going to make a few people seriously unhappy. Probably the same people who care if I use appropriate, upstanding language.

No one should ask you what you want when someone dies. It isn't useful. It isn't helpful. With the exception of wanting my father back, I didn't know what the heck I wanted. For weeks after he died, I felt like my brain was completely submerged in water.

What <u>was</u> helpful:

- One of my high school best friends texted me constantly with messages like "I'm right here when you need someone, no matter what time it is." Because there *will* be a time when you need to tell someone everything, and you need to know there are people who are willing to hear every gory detail. You need people you can call at three in the morning who will not only answer your calls, but will drive over to your house and take care of you, if needed.

- Friends who sent things to the house: flowers, bouquets of fruit, food, etc. I generally hate being sexist, but this may be a girl thing. Nothing says "I love you and I'm here" like fruit on a stick and flowers in a margarita glass. Or the tallest Easter Lily in the free world. I'm not always a "gifts" person, but I will *never* forget the people who sent me gifts during this time period.

- Condolence cards. They are still hard to read, but the best ones have little personal notes in them. And they do help to make you feel like you're not all alone, by yourself, with no one else. Because death strips you of your confidence and your sense of team spirit, and your desire to get out of your pink sweatpants. Not necessarily in that order.

- Personal contact. When someone calls or texts to tell you that they've lost someone in their life, *don't* send them a three-word text back. Don't tell them you're busy. Don't *be* too busy. Drop whatever you're doing for ten minutes and call them. It is the biggest credit to someone else, and to yourself, for you to drop whatever you're doing if even for a brief moment to make their heartbreak your first priority. Nobody controls when their loved one passes away, so people need to know that death and the birth of babies are two phone calls you need to return at 3 a.m., or 10 p.m., or 12 noon. Even if you're at work. Even if you're in an important meeting. Even if it might disrupt your day or your life. Doing the right thing here means everything to someone who's grieving and will be remembered. Doing the wrong thing will, unfortunately, also be remembered.

- The friend who has been there. If you're in the "my loved one has died club," you are uniquely qualified and prepared to understand grief in a way that many other people can't. Which, by the way, is the worst club you'll ever be a member of. Frankly, I'd pay double the dues to get out of this club. My friend who politely warned me not to kill people who were about to say foolish things to me was uniquely qualified because he had lost his mother. He sure didn't ask to be part of the club. He certainly didn't want me to be part of the club. But now, whether he likes it or not, I'm the vice president or the crazy aunt of that club. I'm not sure which. And as a part of your club dues, you pay it forward. Someone will need you to call them and say "Please don't beat anyone who says something stupid to you." Pay your dues. Say it to the next unwilling prospective club member.

- Most of all, speak softly and carry a lasagna. When someone is grieving, what you need to know is that they're largely still polite, although I do occasionally use curse words throughout this process and this book. When you ask what they need, they're most likely going to say, "Nothing...we're just fine."

But the truth is, they're anything but fine.

Even two months after Dad died, heck, even today, almost four years later, I still have moments when the voice in my head is still screaming. But for those first few weeks, I woke up in the middle of the night with night terrors. And a few people knew just what to do. They didn't ask what we wanted.

They just showed up with a lasagna.

This whole "bring food when someone dies" is such a strange tradition. I was raised Protestant and have been a Presbyterian for pretty much my whole adult life. Church people, but Presbyterians in general, are really good at food. They celebrate with cake. Presbyterian Youth Ministry 101 is learning how to cut a sheet cake with dental floss or fishing line. I am not kidding. I learned this skill my second week of youth ministry. They mourn with casseroles. But this whole "bring some food phenomena" is so strange because you generally don't really feel like eating when someone dies. Let alone eating a cheesy noodle or a cheesy potato extravaganza. Make fun all you want, but if you're a church person, don't even *think* of telling me nobody's ever brought you a cheesy noodle or cheesy potato casserole. Or lemon bars. Admit it, church people. Church People 101 is learning to make cheesy potatoes and lemon bars and lasagna. But, whether you feel like eating or not, the kids are still hungry. And if you can't get out of the pink sweatpants, chances are you're not going to the store or feeding anyone.

And so the counter-full of lasagnas began.

People didn't try to talk to us when they dropped the lasagnas off. There was no "Let's talk about Jesus" intro to lasagna-land. Just a simple "We're sorry, here's a lasagna." Bringing lasagnas when someone dies should go down in Presbyterian history as something out of our Book of Order, our book of governing rules. Don't talk. Don't ask if they need help or anything. Just bring a lasagna.

End of story.

Helping someone cope with the death of someone close to them is never easy. But it *is* simple. Make the person still alive feel like you haven't forgotten or deserted them. They already feel forgotten and deserted. Hug them. Hug them again. Hug them ten seconds longer than you should. Don't go for the fancy words. Sit next to them and just listen. Hold their hands. Don't ask what they want or need. Don't use fancy Christian vocabulary, or even assume the person is a Christian. Speak softly and carry a lasagna.

Please note that if you don't know what to say to someone who is grieving, I have included four recipes that will do the talking for you: lemon bars (a staple of Presbyterianism), cheesy tater tot casserole, garlic cheese grits and, of course, lasagna. Oh, and about the garlic cheese grits, don't knock it 'til you've tried it. I was scared to death of grits until I tried these. They taste like dessert. And remember to save your sermon on the mount for another time. Just hand them the casserole and say "I'm so sorry." The friendship you save may be your own.

DO OVER:
Hand over the lasagna. Hug the griever. Back away slowly. Get in your car and drive away. Repeat on a daily basis, or until they have to buy a chest freezer due to casserole overload.

Lasagna Recipe

1 lb. sweet Italian sausage
¾ lb. lean ground beef
½ c. minced onion
2 cloves garlic, crushed
28 oz. crushed tomatoes
13 oz. tomato sauce
12 oz. tomato paste
½ c. water
2 T. white sugar
1 ½ t. dried basil leaves
½ t. fennel seeds

1 t. Italian seasoning
1 T salt
¼ t. ground black pepper
4 T. chopped fresh parsley
12 lasagna noodles
16 oz. ricotta cheese
1 egg
½ t. salt
¾ lb. shredded mozzarella cheese
¾ c. grated Parmesan cheese

Cooking Directions

In a Dutch oven, cook sausage, ground beef, onion, and garlic over medium heat until well browned. Stir in crushed tomatoes, tomato paste, tomato sauce, and water. Season with sugar, basil, fennel seeds, Italian seasoning, 1 tablespoon salt, pepper, and 2 tablespoons parsley. Simmer, covered, for about 1 ½ hours, stirring occasionally.

Bring a large pot of lightly salted water to a boil. Cook lasagna noodles in boiling water for 8 to 10 minutes. Drain noodles, and rinse with cold water. In a mixing bowl, combine ricotta cheese with egg, remaining parsley, and ½ teaspoon salt.

Preheat oven to 375 degrees F (190 degrees C). To assemble, spread 1 ½ cups of meat sauce in the bottom of a 9x13 inch baking dish. Arrange 6 noodles lengthwise over meat sauce. Spread with half of the ricotta cheese mixture. Top with a third of mozzarella cheese slices. Spoon 1 ½ cups meat sauce over mozzarella, and sprinkle with ¼ cup Parmesan cheese. Repeat layers, and top with remaining mozzarella and Parmesan cheese. Cover with foil. Bake in preheated oven for 25 minutes. Remove foil, and bake an additional 25 minutes.

Lemon Bars

Preheat oven to 350 degrees.

BASE:

1 c.	butter or margarine
2 c.	flour
¼ t.	salt
½ c.	granulated sugar

Cut together all base ingredients in a large bowl.
Press into a 9x13 inch pan. Bake for twenty minutes at 350 degrees F.

FILLING:

4	eggs
2 c.	granulated sugar
4 T.	flour
½ t.	baking powder
7 T.	lemon juice

Mix filling ingredients together in bowl. Pour over warm base and return to oven and bake twenty more minutes (top should brown only slightly). Cool at least a short while. Sprinkle/sift with powdered sugar. Cut into squares to serve.

Recipe courtesy of Debbie Bass' mother, Joan Zanfagna.

Garlic Cheese Grits

6 oz.	Pepper Jack cheese
6 oz.	Velveeta
½ t.	garlic powder
¼ c.	butter (½ stick)
1 cup	uncooked grits
1 t.	salt

Preheat oven to 350 degrees F.

Cut cheese into small pieces/chunks.
Bring salted water to a boil; slowly add grits. Bring to a second boil, then reduce heat and cook over medium heat for 4-5 minutes, stirring often so grits don't get lumpy. Turn off heat. Add cheeses, butter and garlic powder to grits. Stir until melted and blended. Pour into a greased 1 ½ quart casserole. Bake uncovered for 30 minutes.

Recipe courtesy of Debbie Bass.
(Adapted from the Junior League of LR, "Little Rock Cooks" Cookbook)

Hash Brown Casserole

32 oz.	frozen hash browns
1 ½ c.	sour cream
1 can	fried onion rings
1 can	cream of chicken soup
2 c.	grated sharp cheddar
½ c.	butter (1 stick)

Preheat oven to 350 degrees.

Melt the butter and pour half in the bottom of a 9 x 13 pan. Break up and arrange the frozen potatoes in the pan. Mix together the sour cream, soup and onion rings. Pour over the potatoes. Sprinkle with the shredded cheddar. Pour the remaining butter over the casserole. Bake uncovered for approximately 1 ½ hours.

Recipe Courtesy Of Debbie Bass, from a friend in Atlanta.

CHAPTER SEVEN

BACON

A short note on grief.

For one entire day while grieving, all I thought about was bacon. In the case of some people, probably including my own children, this probably doesn't seem all that out of the ordinary. There are, in fact, people who love bacon to a fault. Generally speaking, I am not one of those people.

I do like bacon on occasion, but it never consumes my thoughts. But for one whole day, all I thought about was bacon. I thought I smelled bacon everywhere I went. I imagined what bacon donuts would taste like. The answer is....bacon. I imagined my lunch was bacon salad with sprinkled bacon and covered in bacon salad dressing.

In the shower that night, I swear both my shampoo and conditioner smelled like bacon.

I was worried that I might have one of those little known disorders some people have during pregnancy, when professionals say things such as, "Call your doctor if you're ever tempted to eat laundry soap or kitty litter." Can grief cause disorders like this?

Because I most definitely wanted to drink my bacon conditioner. Even though it only smelled like bacon in my twisted, grief-riddled brain. And that's when I knew….for myself…..it was time to seek some professional help. And not from a bacon connoisseur.

DO OVER:

If you ever even contemplate drinking shampoo or conditioner, no matter how delicious it smells, IMMEDIATELY get out of the shower and call your doctor.

CHAPTER EIGHT

PUTTING THE FUN BACK IN FUNERAL

If and when you need to read about a whole new level of funeral event planning, read this.

On a day like any other, I should have been at work. But instead, I was on my way to a funeral service: my father's funeral service. Not only was it particularly inconvenient for everyone, perhaps most of all him, that Dad decided to leave this earth without saying goodbye, but that inconvenience was painfully coupled with his irresponsibility in leaving his last will and testament on his Wednesday to-do list. And then deciding to have a massive heart attack on Tuesday. Which left us with nothing. No plans. No wishes. No party planning directives.

And so the day after he died, my siblings and I met to talk about what his arrangements should look like.

Arrangements. It's such a strange word for something that, in this case, means to "plan a final party that would be fitting for a deceased Scottish, Zen Buddhist/Presbyterian." By that definition, giving everyone we met on the street a couple of Guinness while wearing kilts probably would have sufficed.

I hear funerals and wakes are for the living. This might be true but if it is, people (including us) spend an awful lot of unnecessary time thinking about what the person who has passed away would want for their final party. Because Dad had been a Presbyterian, both his parents had been Presbyterian, and his daughter (me) worked for a Presbyterian church, we had a Presbyterian pastor (my boss) who agreed to do a chapel funeral service in the chapel of the Presbyterian senior citizens home where my great aunt still lived. Because Dad had converted to Buddhism a couple of years before his death, we were able to find the young Zen Buddhist priest from the temple where Dad spent his time, who also agreed to do part of the service. And you cannot be a part of the Wallace clan unless our red plaid tartan is there. Or, without a bagpiper. Hence, the need for Bagpipe Mary.

Have you ever been to a half Presbyterian/half Buddhist funeral? Yeah. Me neither. But I have now. The ritual Christian prayers, hymns, sermons and eulogy were intertwined with a Buddhist funeral service in the middle, which included gong banging and the Zen Buddhist priest chanting while swirling incense through the air. The Buddhist priest started his portion with a loud, guttural yell which, apparently, is customary at Buddhist funerals. There's a reason the Presbyterians are lovingly called the "frozen chosen." We don't clap, we don't wave our hands in the air, and we even have the gall to be occasionally annoyed by anyone who dances during the hymns. We are on our best behavior, especially at funerals. So a guttural yell coming from *anywhere* during a funeral is a moment when you wish you'd had a video camera pointing toward the congregation, just so you could see the largely horrified expressions on everyone's faces. I'd like to share more specific details but, to be honest, I cried through most of the service. Especially the gong banging and incense swirling.

Growing up Protestant, you might not have paid attention during the Sunday school stories featuring Moses, Ruth or Esther. But nobody missed the part about trying to get into heaven. From day one, the goal is to get into heaven. It's Christianity 101.

And throughout the incense swirling and gong banging of Dad's service, I found myself in the midst of a faith crisis. "If what this guy (the Zen Buddhist priest) is doing works, then maybe Dad will come back as a butterfly or a cricket and not bother with going to heaven."

The nonnegotiable idea of getting into heaven is woven into little Christians from the time they're old enough to breathe. And let's face it, as a part of Christianity, Sunday school teachers and pastors (and youth directors: guilty as charged) everywhere sometimes say things they can't possibly prove. Things like, "When you get to heaven, your loved ones will be there," although I'm at least ninety-four percent certain I've never said that.

I may have mentioned that, for reasons unbeknownst to me, Dad didn't call me when he realized he was having a heart attack that day. So I was robbed of the chance to say a few things I really needed to say to him. Not all of them would have been nice. Especially with the not-calling-and-not-going-straight-to-the-doctor thing. So my Christian soul is saving some things I didn't get to say until I get to heaven. I'm holding them in until then. And Dad better be there when I get there, he better clear his schedule. Because that is going to be a very long day.

As the funeral progressed that day, people shared memories of Dad, most of which I don't really remember. Lots of people hugged me, most of which I also don't really remember. And Bagpipe Mary ended the service. A fiery red head, she looked like she had just come from a biker convention, except she was wearing a kilt.

Either I love planning exit parties for people so much, or I just figured we all certainly HADN'T had enough that day, we went straight from the chapel to the cemetery, where the Presbyterian pastor and the Zen Buddhist priest had generously both offered to do their versions of a prayer at Dad's graveside. Here's the part everyone remembers: it was a cold, dreary and windy day. As soon as we arrived at the spot where Dad's ashes were to be buried, it began to rain. It was freezing and rainy and a few people in our group had umbrellas. We placed Dad's urn on the podium provided by the funeral home and each of us, one by one, gently placed roses on top of the urn.

At the very moment the Buddhist priest began to chant, the wind picked up and began howling from all corners of the cemetery. For those of you who think I have an active imagination, I suggest you ask anyone who was there that day. I honestly can't make this stuff up! Almost simultaneously, our umbrellas were all turned inside out by the sheer force of the wind at the same time all the flowers blew off the urn. It was one of those only-seen-in-movies scene. The more the Buddhist priest chanted, the more the wind and rain swirled up, down, and in every direction. More chanting and more swirling. More wind. I had this really strange feeling that if one's soul could brew up a storm, maybe Dad really was there in that moment. I know everyone felt like something out of the ordinary was happening, because most of us were nervously glancing at one another wondering if anyone else was thinking the same thing. And then the Presbyterian pastor said the closing prayer, which we could now barely hear even though we were only a few steps away, because of a hurricane gust of wind at that very moment. And then – just like that – it was over. We left the flowers. We fixed the umbrellas. We left Dad's urn. We left Dad's ashes in that cemetery to be buried in our family plot. We left him, because we had no choice, because he left *us*. I have decided that the cruelest part of a graveside service is when all the cars pull away from the graveside. Maybe because you don't yet realize that you'll never have that moment back. But, even more so, you don't realize that the funeral may be finished, yet the grief is only beginning.

In the days and weeks that followed, more than once I overheard our children tell the story of Dad's graveside service to their friends, complete with tale of the sudden hurricane wind and torrential rain brought on by the Buddhist chanting. To this day, my oldest son fondly refers to that sweet Zen Buddhist priest as "the last Airbender."

CHAPTER NINE

CONVERSATION WITH A BAGPIPER

When grief turns you into a person who willfully has the dumbest phone conversations in the world.

ME: *"Um....I'm looking for a bagpiper. Is this the right number?"*

HIM: *"What kind of a bagpiper?"*

ME: *"Are there different kinds of bagpipers?"*

HIM: *"I mean, for what kind of an event?"*

ME: *"It's for a funeral."*

HIM: *"Oh. I'm so sorry."*

ME: *"How much do you charge to come and bagpipe?"* I'm not sure that word can be used as a verb, but again because of grief, all grammar has fallen by the wayside.

HIM: *"It's about five hundred dollars."*

ME IN MY HEAD: Now I'm the one who's sorry.

HIM: *"What is the date of the event, sweetie?"*

ME: I give him the date.

HIM: *"Sorry, love, I'm busy that day."*

When all sorts of people start calling you "honey" or "love" or "sweetie" at the rate they did after Dad's death, I'm pretty sure it's because they think they're talking to someone who's emotionally fragile. Which only makes the person in question (in this case, *me*) madder and more fragile. At least if you're going to give me a sweet pet name, let me pick it. Tootsie roll? Kewpie doll? Fruit loops? At least that one would be a little more accurate.

ME GETTING FRUSTRATED: *"Well, I have to have a bagpiper! Do you have someone else from your company that you'd recommend?"* At this point, I have convinced myself that I've called some sort of a bagpiper franchise.

HIM: *"Well, it's just me and me pipes."*

If I could have seen through the phone, I'm sure it would have confirmed my suspicions that I was actually talking to the Lucky Charms leprechaun who just happened to play the bagpipes. I really, really wanted to ask him to say "It's magically delicious," but I didn't have the nerve.

HIM: *"But I do know someone, come to think of it!"*

ME: *"You do? Could I have their name?"*

HIM: *"Her name is Mary."*

ME: *"What's her last name?"*

HIM: *"I don't even know, but I have her number. And, in certain circles, she is just known as Bagpipe Mary."* Of course she is. I would expect nothing less.

Be prepared that if you've just hired a woman who is known as Bagpipe Mary in certain circles, don't imagine even for one hot second that this woman is going to look like the grown up version of those adorable little seven-year-old curly red-haired, sweet, feisty Irish dancers. Prepare yourself for someone with a snake tattoo (at least it's Irish...thanks, St. Patrick) who smells like a combination of haggis and whiskey. And who you wouldn't want to meet in a dark alley. Just be prepared.

CHAPTER TEN

URNS AND FOLGERS COFFEE

When grief turns you into a circus monkey who is just trying to be polite.

About two days after Dad's death, I was on the phone with the cemetery where our family plot is located. This cemetery will remain nameless unless someone tells me they're planning to bury a loved one there, in which case, all bets are off.

Because Dad was a Buddhist and had left no final requests, we tried our level best while making all arrangements to do what we thought he would have wanted. To that end, the Buddhists are very into "from the earth and back to the earth," the circle of life, dust to dust, etc. We thought that the best way to make sure arrangements were as he would have wanted was to have his ashes placed in a biodegradable urn before he was buried in our family plot. You know, so he could go "back to the earth."

This real life phone conversation happened between the lady at the funeral home and me.

HER: *"Have you chosen an urn for your father's ashes?"*

ME: *"We have not chosen one yet, because we really want a biodegradable urn. We found some at other locations, but none on the website where you said to look."*

HER: *"That's because you can't have a biodegradable urn."*

Please try to remember that by the time we got to this point, I had spent the night on the phone with the organ donation interrogation squad, the cremation society had lost and then found Dad's body, and I had spent the better part of eight hours scouring the internet for every available bagpiper and a Zen Buddhist priest. And I hadn't slept a wink in two days. Hang onto this information because I'm about to use it as my excuse for poor manners although, in the world of Heather, there really is no excuse.

BRIDEZILLA ME: *"What do you mean we can't have a biodegradable urn? We want a biodegradable urn."* Please refer to the grief version of Bridezilla because, by this point, my manners are being put to the test at an alarming speed.

HER: *"I'm very sorry, ma'am but we don't allow biodegradable urns in our cemetery."* Again, what's with the ma'am thing?! It's not okay in the northern states. How many times do I need to say if someone calls you ma'am in the northern states, you're being addressed as someone who is ninety years old, or older?

ME: *"What do you mean you don't allow biodegradable urns in your cemetery? Why the H-E-double-hockey-sticks not?"*

And here's where the conversation took a serious turn for the worse. Because the difference between what one means to say and what one actually says can be tremendous, especially if the listener is a sleep-deprived, grief-riddled raging lunatic by this point.

WHAT SHE SAID: *"We don't allow biodegradable urns because we require that the deceased be placed in a container they cannot get out of. They need to be contained."*

WHAT SHE ACTUALLY MEANT: *"They don't allow biodegradable urns because Illinois law requires that urns and coffins that are buried be non-biodegradable in case anything ever happens and they need to dig something or someone out of the cemetery."* But she actually said "We don't allow biodegradable urns because we require that the deceased be placed in a container they cannot get out of."

ME: *"Listen lady, in the last three days, my Dad died suddenly. People asked me all kinds of questions about his sex life. They transported him promptly but then lost his body. Then they found him. They cremated him and now he's a pile of ashes. I'm relatively certain that you could put him in a Folger's Coffee can, without a lid, and he couldn't get out of there!"* It is with the utmost shame that I admit that I actually said that. So much for manners. Sorry Mom.

OFFENDED AND HUFFY HER: She was probably rightfully so, but at this point I no longer cared. *"What I meant was that the container the ashes are put in has to be non-biodegradable so it can be removed if necessary."*

ME: *"Whatever. We'll call you back."*

MY BROTHER: *"What was that all about?"*

ME: *"Being that they can't seem to keep Dad contained anywhere, they want to make sure he's in a bin with the lid screwed on tight so his ashes aren't wandering around the cemetery at night. Dad obviously can't be trusted to stay wherever they put him. We can't have a biodegradable urn."*

I made my brother call them back. Luckily we have different last names. So he can pretend not to know me.

Things I Had Nightmares About
While Grieving

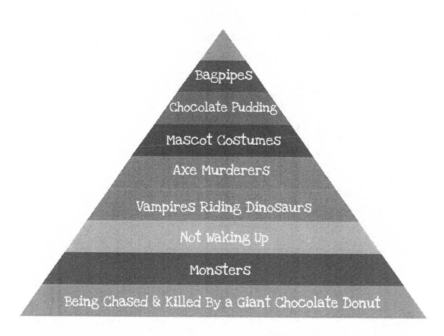

Bagpipes

Chocolate Pudding

Mascot Costumes

Axe Murderers

Vampires Riding Dinosaurs

Not Waking Up

Monsters

Being Chased & Killed By a Giant Chocolate Donut

I suppose, in the scheme of things, if you're going to be chased and killed by something in a nightmare, it's only right that it's something as wonderful and tasty as a chocolate donut.

CHAPTER ELEVEN

ONE, TWO, BUCKLE MY SHOE

When grief turns you into an adult human who can no longer buckle or tie your own shoes.

On the day of Dad's funeral, I was getting dressed just like it was any other day. Actually, I was trying hard to pretend it was just like any other day, but that couldn't have been farther from the truth. In what can only be described as a cruel twist of fate, I could not finish putting on my own shoes. I've heard it said that when someone has a serious injury, like your arm or leg being cut off, other parts of your body stop functioning so your brain and all your body systems can concentrate on the injury. I can only imagine that my grief was consuming all of my brain function and vital body systems at that particular time, in an effort to fight off all the sorrow. I had decided I was going to get through the day completely void of all feeling. I planned to put my emotions in a box, duct tape it, crazy glue it, and nail it shut.

In hindsight, there are lots of things in life that seem like a good idea at the time but don't always go as planned. That "emotion in the duct taped box" may have been one of those ideas.

But I couldn't put on my shoes. More specifically, I couldn't remember *how* to buckle my shoes. I had these cute little strappy heels that had side buckles, but I couldn't remember how to buckle them. My husband watched for a few minutes as I sat on our bed, bent over my shoe, holding the shoe strap in one hand and the buckle in the other – just staring blankly at both.

HIM: *"Are you okay?"*

ME: *"I don't....I can't.....I don't....I can't remember how to buckle these shoes! I can't remember how!"* I am lucky, through this process, to have lived through it with a man that doesn't ask many questions in the face of extreme lunacy.

HIM: *"I got this."* He buckled my shoes.

ME: *"How does someone lose the ability to buckle their own shoes?"*

HIM: *"It will come back."*

It strikes me that, until this moment, I did not think that one's brain or emotional state or ability to buckle their own shoes was something that had to "grow back" like your hair or your fingernails. But he was right. I am happy to report that I can, once again, buckle my own shoes.

In case that's some sort of an important accomplishment in the grand scheme of life.

Or in case you were wondering.

It gets less awful.

DO OVER:
Note to Self: buy Velcro shoes

CHAPTER TWELVE

THE SECOND LETTER

If and when it's been three months since someone passed away, and you are still yelling at them, read this.

Dear Dad,

I wore my real pajamas to bed last night. My real pajamas. Not my sweatpants. Pink sweatpants free for at least four entire weeks. So I don't need a sweatpants 12-step program. No longer needing my pink sweatpants was much to my chagrin, but much to the relief of the man who lives with me, who thought I was destined to split into one of four possible personalities, only three of which would have been acceptable for him to live with on a daily basis. At least one of them was ramping up to wear pink sweatpants, a superhero cape, and a tiara to the grocery store and to visit his mother.

While, on the surface, this superhero sweatpants fashionista look seems like it could be every man's creepy or weird fantasy, it's really not what any full grown male wants in his life or, as it turns out, raising his children. So I learned an important lesson here. Wearing a cape, tiara and sweatpants is acceptable only in one's own living room. Anyway, my letter continues.

And I woke up this morning wondering what the progression of no-longer-needing-the-security-blanket-pink-sweatpants meant. Does it mean I'm going to forget everything that has happened up to this point? Does it mean I'm going to forget what you looked like? Because I'm already starting to have trouble remembering exactly what your voice sounded like. My brain is still pretty cloudy and I feel like I'm starting to forget. And I don't want to. I really don't want to.

Your karate jacket is starting to not smell like you anymore, and I wonder what will happen the day I realize that it actually doesn't smell like you anymore.

Every time I think the "look-how-crazy-this-girl-is" element may finally be a thing of the past, some part of my psyche goes out of its way to prove me incredibly wrong. Last night the "element of crazy" actually physically woke me up in the middle of the night, just long enough that I could crawl out of bed, into my walk-in closet, curl up in your winter jacket, and sobbing myself to sleep on the closet floor.

Someone I recently met, who is absolutely wonderful, told me a story about her experiences after her own father died, and how she got to the point where she couldn't get up in the morning anymore and couldn't stop crying. And that's when she turned to the psychiatric drugs. I'm trying to poll the people I know who have previously been through this and their examples of "....and that's when I took the crazy pills" to make sure I know if I'm ever over that edge and need to admit defeat. Perhaps the next chapters of this book will be happily brought to you by the makers of Cymbalta or some other mood-altering drug. Spoiler Alert: This turns out to be true, later in the book.

Right now my barometers of crazy have become the people closest to me. A couple of them have seen a side of me that isn't so lovely and pleasant. Sometimes I feel like I'm overdosing them on something they didn't sign on for. And that might be my "crazy pill indicator light" going on. Giving someone way more than they can handle might mean you should take the drugs, if that's what is needed, to talk you down I guess.

But, at least this very minute, I'm coping.

A few weeks back, a family member talked to me about a book which defines the major stressors in peoples' lives, and identifies these stressors so that people can either avoid them or figure out what to do when they're in the midst of one of them. I think she said there are like five or six "established human stressors" in the book. Some examples included: death, moving, sending your child off to college, and getting a new job. I don't know what the last one was. This family member's objective, in talking to me about this list, was to point out that I've endured four of these stressors in a three-month period, so maybe I should cut myself a few breaks. I'll bet if I tried really hard, I could probably add whatever that last stressor is onto my list for this same time period. There's some slight possibility that whatever that missing stressor is, maybe I've already lived through that and I'm just not willing to admit it. What I gleaned from this lesson was that all of these things are not supposed to happen or descend upon your universe, like Harry Potter's dementors, all at one time.

Last week someone at work told me they're not sure how I'm still standing. I don't really make jokes about my own mental status too much anymore. Except to say that I'm so glad the man I married found a drive-through liquor hut.

In all seriousness, I really don't do liquid courage. That doesn't work for me. Although grief has put me in a place where, given the right motivation, I'm willing to try. If you've ever had one drink with me, you'd know I don't do liquid courage for a couple of good reasons. I'm not at all morally opposed to drinking in moderation, I'm just not a drinker. And, for every time I do drink, there is a hilarious story left in the wake of that episode. I can't hold my liquor. Sadly, this is a fact, so it's off my list of coping mechanisms.

I am back to fervent list making as a coping mechanism. List upon list. Notebooks of lists. Maybe a whole book of lists this year. Obsessive compulsive list making.

It makes perfect sense that a man who inconveniently died (inconvenient for him AND for me; I'm still mad about this) before finishing his Wednesday "write last will and testament" to-do list would raise at least a couple of children that can't exist without lists to explain how they're going to successfully get a thousand things done in a fourteen-hour period.

I am now juggling not only the to-do lists, but also the "how to fix this" lists.

And the night terrors are back. You used to bring me cups of water when the nightmares got really bad. Last night I got my own water and then fell asleep hugging your jacket in my closet. Yes, it's completely true, I woke up wondering if I'd turned the corner from Crazy Road to Lunatic Avenue in the course of one night.

Today I am just praying for things to go right. I am not trying to live as a saint, a good parent, or a drama queen. I am just trying to survive the day, and I just need to find things to be happy about to help me get through. Which is so weird because on any given day I'm usually the person who can find seven million things to be ecstatically happy about, and I've almost never had to try to be joyful. The glass has always been half full.

I miss you. I miss you in a way that I think is always glaringly apparent on my face. I miss the times when I didn't have to wish that I could undergo regular Botox treatments so my face would be stuck in one expression, instead of feeling like I had to control my sad emotions all the time. I am secretly relieved that the only three people who can read me from across a room, who aren't part of my family, can't see me right now. Because I'm pretty sure they wouldn't have a choice other than to be disappointed in how ridiculous the "trying to act stoic" look appears on me. I'm glad I don't have to try to fool those people who'd know the difference from thirty paces.

I think we all probably have that group. I definitely have that group of three or so people who can bring me to my knees with one look from across the room. I don't bother to try to fool those people. I expect them to keep my secrets and hold my under-eye concealer and not ask questions about why I own a storehouse of cucumbers for the bags under my eyes in case of crying episodes. It's pretty okay, though, because these same people usually don't ask too many questions. I am lucky to have a few people in my life that know what the good and the bad looks like. And who've heard me swear. And who usually know where I put my car keys. Hint: If I'm looking for my car keys, they're probably in my hand.

This morning, my husband told me that I should give myself the benefit of the doubt. From the time I was little, Dad, you gave me lectures about things "that I didn't have the luxury to do." I didn't have the luxury to be a poor student if I wanted to go to college. I didn't have the luxury be a lazy employee if I wanted my employer to rehire me next summer. I didn't have the luxury to not be good at helping take care of all the little people at my house (or my house now) because they were depending on me. I didn't have the luxury of being irresponsible. I didn't have the luxury of being mean. I didn't have the luxury of wasting my life on partying. I didn't have the luxury of falling in love with someone who didn't really love me back. I didn't have the luxury of not preparing for voice lessons or auditions if I ever wanted to be like the other girls in the high school theater department and have the lead in a musical.

Apparently I could have screwed this one up if I wanted to, because the best I was gonna get was a C+ lead in a boring play where I'd be upstaged by a live rooster. True story. I should have traded in the voice lessons for latch hooking or basket weaving, or some other hobby that potentially held less rejection.

I didn't have the luxury. So you see, I learned your lessons, John Wallace. I listened to them, and I learned them well.

I don't have the luxury of the benefit of the doubt. Not now. Not ever. I don't have the luxury of sitting in my closet crying. Nervous breakdowns and grief are supposed to be for those who have that luxury,

I guess. Or at least twenty extra minutes in their day. If you were here, you'd tell me I have a job to do; that much I know for sure.

"Do your job. Unpack your boxes. Take care of the people around you. Do what you're supposed to do."

There's no luxury in grief. You'd tell me to fix what's broken. You'd tell me to figure it out and to not be a quitter and that only sissies cry. Oh, that's my favorite one of your lines to repeat in my head lately! You'd tell me to "pull myself together." You'd tell me to never let the gas gauge in my car get lower than a quarter tank. You'd tell me to keep the jumper cables in my car. You'd tell me that I didn't have the luxury to depend on someone else to save me or fix things. It's funny because sometimes you'd tell me that while you were changing my tire or the oil in my car. Irony. It wasn't lost on me, Dad. You wouldn't tell me to give myself the benefit of the doubt. And I'm not going to. I'm going to try to fix things. I don't know how. But at least I'm going to make a list.

Love,

Heather

CHAPTER THIRTEEN

THE F WORD

If and when you find yourself needing vocab words that probably shouldn't come out of your mouth in polite conversation with other human beings, read this.

I deplore the F word. At least I thought I did, before Dad died. What I have learned about myself over the last few months is just when you think you've got yourself almost under control, God, or fate, or Buddha, or Zeus, or whatever magic genie you believe in, steps forward with the power to full out and, sometimes rather painfully, morph you into something completely unrecognizable.

For me, it's God. I believe in God. I consider myself a believer in God, although truthfully I'm more of a "doubting Thomas" than I am a person of blind faith. And those beliefs have, with very few exceptions, been tested with Dad's passing. What I'm learning through grief is that God and I have a love/hate relationship. I'm sure God loves me, but I can't always return that love. I rarely fall in a category that could be considered a middle, peaceful ground. If I love you, I love you. If I hate you, I hate you. I can't be lukewarm about God or about most people in my life. So sometimes I have no choice but to really, really hate God. Many God-fearing Christians would suggest that a mantra like that has gotten better people than

I thrown into a lion's den, into the belly of a great fish, or turned into pillars of salt. I'll take my chances. There are probably a host of people, probably also better than I am, who would love to judge my relationship with God and suggest it should be much deeper than the occasional battle of love versus hate. But I'm guessing that those who would be the first to judge probably haven't had an all-out pudding-crying episode.

Shortly after Dad passed away, I stopped eating ice cream. I couldn't eat it. It had always been one of our favorite things, and now it sometimes makes my stomach churn just to look at it. After two or three really awful stomach-churning episodes, I decided to instead try a bit of chocolate pudding. On my first post-funeral challenge with the pudding, there was so much crying that the entire ordeal caused me to almost choke to death on three heaping teaspoons of chocolate pudding. Oh, sure, it's funny *now*, but I put my head down on the table, right into my bowl. True story. My head was fully immersed in a bowl full of delicious chocolate pudding.

The entire time I was choking, all I could think about was "What kind of a God lets someone die without saying goodbye? What kind of a God lets someone die with unopened gallons of Breyers' ice cream in his freezer? What kind of a God lets a soccer mom die from a choke-tastic bowl of chocolate pudding? What kind of a God gave me enough free will to try to eat chocolate pudding in my fragile mental state? F#$%. F#$%. F#$%. F#$%."

I instantly have a few extra modicums of respect for you if, while reading my creative swearing, your human brain translated the last four words into "fish, fish, fish, fish."

I think until one has cried a huge puddle of tears into their own pudding, so much so that you ended up eating the bowl full of tears mixed with equal parts chocolate pudding because of your heartbreak over the loss of another human being, you should really think twice before judging anyone else. And once you've been in a state like that, you know better than to judge *anybody* for *anything*.

And it's for moments like these that I now reserve the right to use the F word.

"Deplorable!" you say? I completely agree. I was certainly raised better than that. Even being raised by wolves prepares you for better than the "mother of all cuss words." Most of us were raised better than that. I reserve the "people who regularly say the F word conversationally" category for people who generally look like the troll guarding the bridge in the Billy Goats Gruff story, or for people whose intelligence ranks slightly higher than gelatin and pond scum. But maybe slightly lower than belly button lint. So while I'm busy not judging people (dripping sarcasm), I'll make sure to add myself to the list of ignorant humans who feel the need to use the F word without ceasing. But, since grief and crying in my pudding is no longer a scenario that only happens to other people, and is now a reality in my own life, it seems that saying the F word on a semi-regular basis is never that far off.

You never know when shooting out a phrase like "Oh, for f#$%'s sake," won't be just the thing that's needed to get someone's attention while you're grieving. Or to make them laugh.

I still like to reserve the F word for special occasions as much as possible. Not holidays though. Because ever since Dad passed away, during major holidays I much prefer to sit in a corner and breathe deeply into a brown paper bag. But you never know, I may decide to crack out into a full out "f#$% you" (translation for the PG-13 crowd: *"fish you"*) splendor on Thanksgiving day, right between the time when I find out someone ate all my ice cream and when I realize my jeans are definitely not going to fit the next day.

We had one Thanksgiving gathering when my youngest sister thought it would be a good idea to have everyone write down one thing they were thankful for on a slip of paper. In all fairness to her, it was a good idea for any normal family, but she seriously underestimated the depths of crazy she was dealing with. All the slips of paper went into a bowl, and each person picked one out at random, read it aloud to the group, and then we talked about each one and tried to guess who wrote the "thankful" suggestion. In a family that takes themselves far too seriously, this might have been an amazing activity centered on spirituality and fraught with thankfulness and blessings. We are not that family. Raised by wolves. Sorry, mom. Leave it to our extended family and friends to include things like strippers and string cheese in the mix of things they're thankful for. And sometimes, when grief gets me down, I thank God for strippers, string cheese, and the unadulterated use of the F word when I need it.

I hope this part of my personality is temporary. Less than temporary. Because the F word doesn't sound pretty or educated coming out of even the most scholarly individual's mouth. So, for *fish's* sake, I hope it goes away. Sooner rather than later.

DO OVER:
Find your own creative word that ISN'T a cuss word. One of my interns uses the phrase "cheese and rice" in lieu of taking the Lord's name in vain.
Credit to Maggie Johnson

CHAPTER FOURTEEN

HAIKUS ON GRIEF

When grief turns you into a poor, disgraceful excuse
for a poet.

For one whole day after Dad died, I wrote haikus about death in my head. But I started with this one, because it was the only thing I could come up with for about five hours. I apologize in advance to every English and poetry teacher I've ever had, as well as people who really care about etiquette and decorum. I'm sorry. And advance apologies to the wolves who raised me to know better than this. I'm sure this page alone will get me banished from the wolf pack. As it should.

Unhelpful haiku/reasons I've largely stopped cussing: It doesn't fix or solve anything.

S$%^, $#$%, $%^&, $%^&, $%^&

#$%^, $%^&,#$%^, #$%^, $%^&, $%^&, #$%^

#$%^, @#$%, #$%^, #$%^, #$%^

This was about the time I asked my doctor if they still do electroshock therapy on people. Because I really don't want to be an utter disappointment, especially to the wolves who raised me.

For one whole day, I wrote "death" haikus, in my head. Maybe because I was grieving. Maybe because I took too many poetry seminars in college and I desperately needed to prove that I could put them to good use.

Death comes whispering
It steals your joy, breaks your heart
You are there, then gone

Grief and baseball bats
Beat you up and bully you
Take your lunch money

Death is full of things
It makes you forget people
You forget yourself

On the other side
Is a life of loveliness
If grief can let go

Death makes people weird
They forget the path they're on
Coming back is hard

Death is so awful
Stay here with me: don't go
I can't let it go

After reading all of my wonderfully, carefully crafted haikus on death and grief, including the first one, which was really just a slew of curse words in 5-7-5 format, my husband suggested that perhaps haikus weren't my thing.

Does that mean he didn't like them?

You be the judge.

He suggested instead that perhaps there's a more positive outlet that would fill this need for a combination of poetry and grieving.

He suggested that I switch to writing limericks.

Maybe I will, as soon as I can come up with one that doesn't have the word "Nantucket" in it. Because he suggested that those often don't end well, either.

Maybe poetry's not my thing.

DO OVER:
If, instead of poetry, cussing starts coming through your pen, consider working out at the gym, painting, singing or some other outlet as a viable alternative to writing...at least for a little while.

HAS GRIEF MADE ME CRAZY?
- A HELPFUL FLOWCHART -

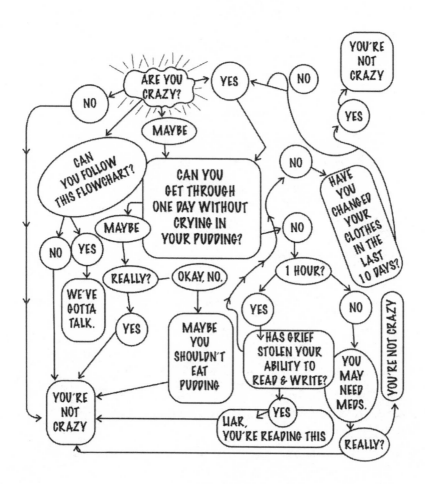

CHAPTER FIFTEEN

ORGAN DONATION

If and when you need to know about organ donation, from the next of kin perspective, read this.

One of the hardest moments in the few weeks immediately following my dad's death was when I received a medal in the mail. It wasn't for me. It was for him. But they sent it to me as the next of kin, along with a letter about my "thank you gift." It was a bronze medal inscribed with the words *Gift of Life Donor*. This is my dad's trophy for donating his organs.

The package arrived with a medal and a thank you certificate. For my wall. Or something like that. I wonder if people actually keep this stuff. Is the certificate supposed to be a good conversation piece for your living room wall? "Yeah...ya' see that? My dad. He died. He was an organ donor. No big deal. I got a medal because he was a donor, too. Wanna see it?"

My dad, in his usual fashion, did everything in his own unique way right up to death. He didn't give us time to prepare, to be ready, or quite frankly to be anything but shell-shocked. He went quickly, and I am left with the aftermath of grief and learning how to deal with that. We never talked about organ donation. I never even knew he was an organ donor, or that the organ donor box was checked on his drivers' license. For the record, I am a big fan of being an organ donor. I was raised that once you're gone, you don't need to return to your body, and I've had friends for my whole life who are waiting for the most serious of transplants. I would do anything to play a part in keeping those friends alive, so I've always been an advocate for organ donation. When you know people who are waiting for a transplant, that choice is relatively easy to make. When you know someone who is waiting for a heart, liver or a kidney, you're more likely to check that donor box. More than likely, a complete stranger will ultimately be responsible for saving your loved one's life. But the reality is, most of the time, someone has to die before your loved one gets an organ they need to live.

In my dad's case, because of all of the drugs they pumped into his body while trying to resuscitate him multiple times, most of his organs were no longer viable for transplant. But lest I get ahead of myself, let me tell you how the organ transplant process works. Because someday you might need to know.

This is what happened the night my father died.

On April 3, my sister called around 6:30 pm to tell me Dad had suffered a heart attack. She said they were trying to fix it, and we should be able to see him soon. My other sister and I hurried to the hospital, only to hear the news get worse and worse and worse. My dad never woke up. And in those moments, time began to slip away from me. In the endless night that followed, and the endless nights that have haunted me since, one begins to understand how zombie movies are written. I now know what a real zombie looks like: a soul-less, non-feeling creature that roams the earth only occasionally eating and never sleeping. Grief made darn sure that I know what *that* feels like.

And so in the whirlwind of the night my father died, we saw our dad right as his life was ending, signed papers and, after my sister had a fist fight with the hospital parking voucher machine (we were all pretty out of our minds), we all went home. I apparently sent three text messages from the hospital. I have no memory of sending them. I wore my shoes up to my bedroom, which hasn't happened since I was in elementary school. I collapsed on my bed, shoes still on. And then the phone rang. It was after midnight. It was the organ donation society on the phone.

In the moments since my dad's death, I have added new things to the list of jobs I would never want to have. Working for the organ donation society is *definitely* on that list. Within a two-hour span after my dad's death, they had an organ donation society representative calling me on the phone, informing me that Dad had indicated on his driver's license that he wanted to be an organ donor. This representative told me that, in order for this organ donation to happen, there were questions that needed to be answered right away. I was then informed that the answering of these questions would take forty-five minutes. It really didn't matter how long the questions took, because I no longer had anywhere to go or be, and no understanding of how this could have happened. In those moments, I completely lost track of space and time. So I compliantly agreed to answer the organ donation questions over the phone. I somehow found my wolves-raised manners, and I politely said, "Go ahead." At this point, shortly before 12:30 am on April 4, I had nothing left except politeness. There was still politeness. Somehow I was able to remember how to "do" politeness. Being raised by wolves isn't all bad.

My dad and I never discussed his wishes regarding end-of-life issues. I could tell you that he wanted to go to karate camp and what kind of ice cream he liked. I could tell you how much he liked Pepsi. I could tell you what he thought the best movie ever made was. But talking about mortality is far less fun to talk about than talking about going to the dojo, so I don't have the faintest clue what his final wishes were.

I woke up in the early morning hours wondering if my dad, wherever he was, knew I was making end-of-life choices for him. And if he wasn't somewhere howling all of the following.

1. *No!* For the love of all things holy, don't let *her* be the one to make these decisions! She can't even decide what kind of breakfast cereal she likes!
2. *Ian! I want Ian to make this decision!* [my younger brother] *He knows what kind of breakfast cereal he likes!*
3. *Or Erin! Pick Erin!* [My younger sister] *She's in charge! She's calm! She's responsible!*
4. *Or Meghan! Please pick Meghan!* [My youngest sister] *She managed a company! She's capable of making tough decisions!*
5. *But not her! Not that one! She can't even get out of her own subdivision without a GPS or a completely written out map! She can't decide this! Pick anyone else in the room! Do eeny-meeny-miney-mo!*

I wonder if he'd be so disappointed with the decisions I made in the weeks after his death, and if he'd say he loved me but didn't like my choices.

If he had been conscious, I wonder if he would have grabbed a pencil and written, "Let someone who's not going to have an ongoing meltdown make this decision." Or maybe "Not *that* girl. She was voted by this group to be most likely to need antidepressants in the future if she has to decide something life-changing or be someone's next of kin. Let's vote *her* off the island. *Who's with me?*" or "Wait....*what* did you get on your ACT again?" For the record, I am the first of six children, five of whom are close to genius level according to the ACT, and according to everyone who knows them. And *one* of whom sometimes forgets how to buckle her own shoes. "Let's give someone who got a little closer to a perfect score on the ACT make life and death decisions for me, shall we?" But he never told me anything. *He didn't have a chance to.*

So when the organ donation society employee told me that Dad had indicated he wanted to donate his organs, I felt like I finally had one chance to do what he wanted.

Finally.

One chance.

What you need to know, if you're ever in this situation, is that the well-meaning person responsible for calling you in the middle of the night regarding your loved one's organs has a battery of questions. A *battery* of questions. Not just two. Not just five. And they're not multiple choice. You need to know that no guidebook can prepare you for these questions. Someone needs to tell you in advance that when your brain is the least likely to function properly, you will have to answer these questions. All of them.

These questions included an inquiry about whether my dad may have visited a list of little known countries in the 1980s, which are apparently places one could have contracted dreaded diseases or been, at the very least, chased by Ebola-infected monkeys. Shockingly, the organ donation society doesn't want to transplant human organs if there is a forty percent chance you may have Ebola. After listening to the lady rattle off some of the countries and their virus opportunities, I wondered if tourists visiting some of these countries realize that there are ridiculously scary and life-threatening diseases running rampant in those places. Mostly through monkeys and mosquitos, apparently. I also didn't know I was going to need a map, a world atlas or a globe to answer most of the questions, and not because I got only a B+ in geography. Some of these places were *that* obscure.

The questions continued, delving into details about whether or not my dad had any symptoms of either mad cow disease or bubonic plague. I didn't even know that bubonic plague was still a "thing." Just in case, the organ procurement lady tells you the symptoms, so you can contemplate at length whether or not your loved one was exhibiting any of the symptoms. The symptoms of mad cow (the part of it that humans can contract) include tingling sensations in parts of the body, inability to walk, and psychotic behavior. My dad had six kids. Anyone who has six kids occasionally exhibits psychotic behavior. It has nothing at all to do with mad cow disease.

One section in this Spanish Inquisition-esque battery of questions on *Today's Fun with Grief*, starring my dad and his now emotionally regressed eldest daughter who was lucky enough to be his next of kin, included questions about exactly what types of medicines my dad was taking before his death. Lucky for me, my younger sister handed me Dad's personal effects that night. So I got to throw the contents of his backpack on my bed and sort through the vials of medicine. Not so lucky for me, my dad didn't want to carry around too much stuff. He had taken empty pill bottles, stripped the labels off, and relabeled each with one big letter on the top of each vial. Don't try this at home. There was one bottle with a letter S, one with a letter R, and one with a letter M. I asked the lady on the phone if she was familiar with a little white pill that started with the letter S. And so on, and so forth. It was an *exceptionally* fun game that added to an already truly *terrific* night. Because I am still having trouble letting go of my dad and his things, I kept one of the empty medicine bottle with the letter S on the top. I carry it around with me. It has Motrin in it. My kids, my husband, and now my readership all know that the S bottle is for *Motrin*, just in case I die and you need that info to donate my organs. Please don't ask me why I didn't keep the M bottle for Motrin; let's just stick with the knowledge that grief plays funny tricks on people which includes taking away their ability to be very forward thinking or to use their good common sense.

The next series of questions the organ lady asked was if my dad was a frequent needle-drug user, or if he exchanged sex for drugs or money. I don't know for sure, but my dad did live through the 1960s so I've seen enough flower child meets Puff the Magic Dragon movies to believe that anything is a possibility. But I did almost vomit during this part of the battery of questions. Twice.

The last set of questions were about my dad's sexual history. In the kingdom of Heather, the words "Dad," "sexual," and "history" do not *ever* have any business being in the same sentence. Aw H*&^, if you've read this far, you should already know that the word "sexual" by itself is enough to cause me to freak out to the point of having to wash my brain out with soap. These words don't belong together in my book. Not anywhere.

The lady had questions about sex, sexual partners, gay sex, and sex for money. They wanted numbers, data, and dates. I had one moment when I was actually somewhere between vomiting and passing out. And seriously considered taking a handful of whatever was in the pill bottle labeled with the letter S. It was probably only Motrin anyway. I only wish that someone had told me in advance that, while in this frame of mind, I was going to be expected to answer these questions. It might have lessened the blow. So I'm telling *you*.

Maybe you think this info shouldn't be in a book somewhere. If you ask me, these questions shouldn't be out anywhere in the real world. But someday, if someone you love dies, and I hope they never do, the organ donation society is required to ask these questions. Try to remember they're just doing their job. Try to remember that you can save someone's life by answering the questions. Try to remember not to let the world shake you or change you. I hope your politeness also kicks in.

For about thirty seconds, I had to think about the number of sexual partners that my dad might have had in the last ten years. I didn't know. But immediately after his death, I became the same emotional age as a three year old. I sat on my husband's lap, cradled in his arms, rocking back and forth in a fetal position. So when you ask a forty-something, who has emotionally regressed to the age of her preschool self, about her Dad's sexual history, *nothing* good can come of that. *Nothing. Not a thing.* I answered, "I don't know." And my husband graduated, at that moment, to holding my hand as I sucked the thumb on my other hand.

Two years before Dad's death, his vision was getting progressively worse. He talked about it quite a bit, because when one's vision starts to go, it's hard to do karate. And boy oh *boy*, did he love karate. I don't know exactly when he latched onto this phrase, but he liked to tell everyone that he had "lost his binocular vision." When our kids asked how he was doing, he'd say he couldn't compete at karate tournaments anymore because he had lost his binocular vision. Our kids thought it was cute and funny, in a Mr. Miyagi from *The Karate Kid* kind of way. But that night, on the phone with the organ lady, she said they were interested in harvesting Dad's eyes for patients who need cornea replacement, and his healthy arm and leg bones, which can apparently be used to help patients with certain types of cancer. And all I could say, over and over again to the lady on the phone was that "he had lost his binocular vision." As if that mattered.

I suppose, in the scheme of things, it's nice to think that someone who had lost their sight might now have those beautiful Scottish Keebler elf blue eyes, with or without the binocular vision.

I can't help but hope that some karate-loving nine year old received my dad's eyes, and has had to hone his other skills to compensate for his loss of binocular vision. My dad would have been so pleased and proud to have been a part of some little kid's karate journey that included overcoming adversity or "using the force, Luke." Star Wars: always cite your source!

Because my dad chose to be cremated (at least he told one of us that much), the next day I had to call the cremation society to arrange to have him transported from the organ donation society to the crematorium. And about a week after that, the mail came.....

The package arrived containing the bronze medal inscribed with the words *Gift of Life Donor*. And the tears came. I made my husband put it in a box somewhere, where I won't be likely to run across it on an average day, thus disturbing the balance of power that is my now delicate psyche. I can't stand to look at it. I threw up when it came in the mail. They should give you the medal when you sign up to *be* an organ donor. It really is important to be an organ donor, and one deserves an award for volunteering. But to send it to the grieving family member who's trying to say the right thing and not lose her mind over the smallest details seems a little like cruel and unusual punishment.

"Hey Dad!! You got another trophy. Good job! It's like a gold star, except way heavier. I think you would have preferred an engraved can of Pepsi. And we know we'd both have preferred a gallon of Breyer's ice cream in the mail."

DO OVER:

While I'd rather never get a medal like that in the mail again, I can't do this one over. Donate your organs. Encourage others to donate theirs. Put it on your driver's license. Tell your family your wishes as far as organ donation; there are plenty of wonderful people in this world who will be able to use your loss as another chance at life.

Do NOT Say These Things
To Someone Who IS
Grieving....

It's God's plan.

They're in a better place.

God needed another angel.

Someday this will all make sense.

They wouldn't want you to be sad.

Hang on to the memories. It will get better.

I know how you feel/I know how you're feeling.

God never gives you more than you can handle.

God gives his hardest battles to his strongest soldiers.

You should be happy because they're no longer suffering.

For loss of a child: At least you have other children.

They lived a good long life. You should be thankful.

For loss of a spouse: You're young; you can find someone else.

For loss of a parent: At least you haven't lost both of your parents.

You need to get out of the house.

Try to keep yourself busy.

Try not to think about it.

You have to move on.

This too shall pass.

It's better this way.

It was their time to go.

Time heals all wounds.

You need to get over it.

You're being prepared for something better.

Grief must be teaching you something you needed to learn.

Do you need anything? HINT: They don't know what they need. jump in and do something!

Call me if you need anything. HINT: Do not say this unless you 100% mean it and aren't going to back out.

Grief divided is made lighter

CHAPTER SIXTEEN

MINIONS AND THE BEE GEES

If and when you need one moment to laugh at someone else's misery, read this.

Death, specifically preparing for someone else's death, should come with a manual. I suppose if it's your own death, you don't need the manual, because however you handle your own passing is going to be okay, and people will remember you fondly. But coping with someone else's death, expected or unexpected, should come with a manual. Or at least a really solid "choose your own ending" book. Or a flow chart. But who am I kidding? Death is always unexpected. Even if you see it coming, you still hold out hope for one miracle that might materialize when you need it most.

If you loved someone yesterday, and today they had the nerve to end up dead without discussing it with you first, and without preparing you for the ensuing firestorm you have to deal with, there should really be a manual. Stories about organ donation and cremation should be part of that manual, just in case you need to know any of those little details.

My dad donated his organs. He didn't tell us how or where he wanted to be buried, or if he wanted his ashes sprinkled on Mars or at the circus or a botanical garden. He did check the box on his driver's license indicating organ donor. It was a great way of telling us his wishes by not *actually* telling us his wishes. And, by great, I mean completely terrible. We were all about his wishes. His organs were donated. We didn't know that with organ donation you get a free ride to wherever you are being buried or cremated. Helpful tip: If you are an organ donor, your body's transportation is paid for after your organs are harvested. Is it completely wrong and inappropriate for me to be angry that it takes donating one's organs for any part of the funeral process to be free? My dad was Scottish to a fault, and liked to save money. As an added bonus, he was a bus driver and often made deals or bartered with organizations who couldn't afford busing. So I take solace in the fact that I'm sure he was thrilled that his final transportation was free.

The organ donation organization harvested what they felt were viable parts of my dad's body, with some detail to his leg and arm bones and his eyes. I know these things because they, the powers that be, call first and then send a certified letter letting you know what body parts they took. I'm not sure why. In my dad's case, they had valiantly fought to keep him alive after the heart attack. Which meant that most of his internal organs were unusable due to all the drugs they used to try to save his life. Personally I'm quite glad Dad's heart wasn't harvested. I've heard stories about people who underwent a heart transplant, and then their personality transformed to that of the donor.

I am already damaged enough to stalk people who, like my dad, wear socks with sandals. I believe I could have been permanently damaged by feeling the need to ask every potential stranger in my future if his or her favorite movie was *Citizen Kane*, Dad's favorite movie, as independent confirmation of a heart transplant from my dad, had they taken his heart.

After they took his organs, the organ donation society promptly transported him to the cremation society, who will remain nameless, unless one of my friends plans to have a loved one cremated there, in which case all bets are off. Why? Because the cremation society promptly lost Dad. His body. They lost Dad's body. Here is the ensuing phone conversation:

ME: [Baby sighs from crying, for dramatic effect, and because it actually happened this way. I'm an ugly crier.] *"My dad died about two days ago and the organ donation society called to let us know that his body has been transported there. I needed to call and confirm when his ashes will be ready to be picked up. His name is...was...is... [I'm still unsure what tense you use in this case)] John Wallace."*

CREMATION SOCIETY MINION EMPLOYEE: *"Hmmmmm. I'm looking in my system and don't have a record of him being here."*

ME: [The baby sighs have stopped and the ninja fighting is beginning in my brain. These small ninjas have swords and whiffle bats.] *"What do you mean you don't have a record of him? Did you spell our last name right? They just called me from the organ donation society and told me he's there. They definitely dropped him off."*

MINION: *"Let me check again."* I can hear furious typing, even over the sound of smoke coming out of my own ears and over the gasping, hyperventilating breaths that I'm now taking. *"Hmmm....Nope, no record. Are you sure they took him to this cremation society?"*

In my head, I'm carefully considering the fact that this woman clearly thinks I'm crazy. Also carefully considering the fact that she's talking to me as if cremation societies are as common as McDonald's and tanning salons.

HER: *"Could it have been the north side location? You know, honey, the one by Walmart?"* It's a cremation society, for Pete's sake. Yes, I know which one I called.

ME: *"Yes, I'm certain they brought him there. I checked with the people at the organ donation society, and they gave me your address and your number."*

MINION: [Sighs loud enough so I can hear her.]

Now both of my personalities are together, the voice in my head, and the Other Me who doesn't speak aloud for fear of hulking out on someone: Did she really just sigh at me? Oh no she didn't! She sighed at me! She did!

MINION: *"Well, it seems as though he's not here right now."*

HULK ME: *"Where the #$%^ IS he? Did he go out for coffee? They already took his arms and legs and eyes. Did he decide that jogging and karate were too much of a stretch, but maybe a good cup of tea was worth escaping for?"*

KINDERGARTEN TEACHER ME [Like I used to do when my daughter was a toddler and would misplace her shoes]: *"Let's go back and think about where the last place he might have been would be. Where do you remember seeing him last? Where do they normally place bodies when they are delivered?"*

Now I'm furious, being that I've used the term "bodies" and "delivered" to describe my dad, who I still consider a person and not an object. And who I am still angry at for having the nerve to be deceased. I'm not sure my dad was all that pleased about the whole dying suddenly thing either, since he still had the good, high quality ice cream unopened in his freezer, so I'm guessing he was hoping his Tuesday would have ended differently as well, but I sometimes like to make grief "all about me."

ME: *"What do you mean he's not there? Where could he have gone?"*

MINION: *"Ma'am."*

HULK ME: Now she's sighed at me and called me "ma'am" which, again, in the north is the same as addressing your ninety year old grandmother in a sassy way. You are now two strikes in, lady. In the south ma'am is generally all about respect, but in the north if you're not ninety, nobody calls you ma'am unless they want to get their butt kicked.

MINION: *"Ma'am. I didn't mean he's gone anywhere. I'm sure he's here somewhere, but we may have just temporarily lost him."*

When someone dies, do not tell the loved ones of the individual in question that you've "lost him." Temporarily or otherwise. Contrary to popular belief, this does not inspire confidence. It also serves as an additional opportunity for someone who is already desperately fighting their temper to go bat sh%^ crazy on you.

HULK ME AND ACTUAL ME: *"You lost him?"* [Sorority girl inhale, sorority girl huffy prissy exhale.] *"What do you mean you lost him?"*

MINION: *"I'm sure he's just misplaced."*

HULK ME: *"As if that's somehow better."*

MINION: *"If you'll hold on just a moment, I'll go check and see if he's here. Could you tell me what he looks like?"*

ME: *"What the....??"* Translation: What the FISH?? Regaining my composure, *"Um....He's kinda short and has white hair and sticking out of his ears. And he looks kinda like the Keebler elf."* People told me all my life that this was completely true about my dad.

ME: To my husband who is standing next to me, listening to the conversation, with his mouth gaping open, *"Should I include the part where he's probably missing his eyes and arms and legs and may, by this point, fit into a shoebox?"*

MY HUSBAND, WHO HAS GOOD MANNERS, LOVES ME, DOESN'T LIKE IT WHEN PEOPLE ARE IMPOLITE JERKS, ESPECIALLY ME: *"Heather, leave that part out. I know you're upset. So do they."*

ME: *"He's short, has white hair and looks like a sweet little elf."* [Burst of crying]

My dad looked like the Keebler elf. I'm not exaggerating. My friends always said so. He had the cutest curly white hair and sticking out ears and skinny little bird legs, and twinkly blue eyes and a big smile. In fact, he looked so much like a Keebler elf that people would have been happy to eat cookies out of a tree, had they been served by him. That's how good the resemblance was. But I wasn't in a good place to give good descriptions to anyone by this point in the day. And, by this point in the day, I mean *9:30 am.* When this kind of conversation precedes your morning coffee, be cognizant of the fact that the rest of the day will probably not be all that stellar and wonderful.

ME STARTING OVER: *"Um, he was kind of thin and not very tall and had white hair. And he is missing his arm bones and leg bones and his eyes."* I really said this, because I was hysterical from three days of crying. This is where I started choking from crying and also from karma, I think, for being rude to someone who I felt richly deserved it.

MINION: *"If you'll just hold on, I'll go check for him."*

In the seven and a half minutes I was on hold, I listened to the Bee Gees, their choice of hold music. I will never, ever, *ever* again be able to listen to the Brothers Gibb and "How Deep is Your Love." Never again.

The following thoughts ran through my head during that seven and a half minutes on hold:

1. Is the cremation society like the morgue on *Law and Order SVU*? Are the people in drawers? Did they just "shelve" him wrong?
2. Is it possible my dad talked the organ donation society taxi/hearse driver into one final drive-thru restaurant joyride to get a Pepsi? I would have expected nothing less of my father.
3. Did they leave him somewhere? Was he in some abandoned hallway waiting for someone to find him?
4. Where the H#$% was he?
5. How does someone lose my dad?
6. Why, why, *why* was their hold music the Bee Gees? I *hate you*, Barry Gibb. Stop wondering how deep my love is . . . and *find* my dad!
7. Were there six oompa loompas on the other end of the phone frantically opening and slamming file drawers, trying to figure out which guy looked the most like the Keebler elf?
8. My dad liked to call himself the "karate ninja." Is it possible, in one last attempt to boggle our minds, he actually *escaped* from the grips of these obviously incompetent people?

This is the part where I'll be completely frank with you: Nobody loses my dad. You might have wanted to while he was talking your ear off, but you just didn't. He knew his way around. Everywhere. Getting lost wasn't really something that he did. That was for other people. He drove people around in buses before there was MapQuest or GPS. He didn't get lost. For sure he lost *other* people. He once lost one of my sister's toddlers for hours while he was supposed to be watching him. My sisters were both beside themselves when that happened. He didn't always watch his grandchildren as carefully as we expected him to. But he never got lost all on his own. So to pull this kind of stunt after death overwhelmed, surprised and seriously aggravated me.

And then, almost as quickly as one can say "Jive Talkin'," the lady minion was back on the phone. I now loathe those Brothers Gibb, seemingly through no fault of their own, just bad timing.

MINION: *"Good news! We found him! He's here."*

As if finding a man who has been deceased for two days and has had his arms, legs and eyes removed is some sort of an academic achievement, like winning an award for the science fair.

ME: *"Thank goodness. What a relief. I'd hate for him to be running around without his eyes and limbs. If you could just hang onto him until this afternoon so we can pick him up, that would be great. Try not to let him run away."* Again, I apologize, but the usual polite filter is only now starting to come back. Sorry, not sorry.

ME IN MY HEAD: Have you ever had anyone lose your dry cleaning? I have. When that happens, the dry cleaning business pays you the full value of your clothing if they lose or wreck your clothing. I was trying to decide in my head what to ask for in exchange, if they had permanently lost my dad. Something like: "Aw h#$%, that's okay… just gimme any old ashes." Or maybe, "I'd like the equivalent value of my dad, but I want it delivered, all in chocolate coins, to the following location."

ME: *"When can we pick up his ashes?"*

MINION: *"Could you tell me your name again, and your dad's name?"*

ME: [Face palm. Times seven million.]

DO OVER:
Isn't this what "toe tags" are for? And since they had harvested my dad's leg bones and he probably no longer had toes to tag, would it have been too much to ask that they stick a "Hello my name is……" nametag on him?

CHAPTER SEVENTEEN

NOT THAT ZEN

When grief turns you into the person who, yet again, has the dumbest phone conversations in the world.

ME: *"Ummmm....I'm looking for a Zen Buddhist priest. Do you have any of those at your location?"*

I felt like I was calling a department store to have them put something on hold for me. Can you just deliver me your nearest Zen Buddhist priest? Or I can pick him up at your location later today? Or will you have UPS deliver him to my location?

HER: *"We do. Is there something I can help with?"* I could be wrong here, but I'm pretty sure she wanted to laugh.

ME: *"My father recently passed away. He belonged to a Zen Buddhist temple. But we don't know which one."*

HER: *"Oh I'm so sorry. What was your father's name?"*

ME: *"John Wallace."*

HER: *"Well, that name doesn't sound familiar, but if you hang on for just a minute, I will ask a few other people."*

Their hold music was very Zen elevator music. I was just so relieved that it wasn't the Bee Gees.

HER: *"I'm very sorry for your loss, but nobody here seems to have known your dad. I can give you the numbers for seven other Buddhist temples that are in this area and you could call them and hopefully one of them will be able to help you."*

This was probably the only time, during this entire process, that I was glad my dad was a Buddhist. I cannot even begin to imagine how many Catholic or Baptist or Presbyterian churches are in the greater Chicagoland area that I would have had to call to find the right one, had he been a Christian.

ME: "Thank you so much."

Anyone want to hazard a guess how many times I had to have this same conversation with people at *other* Buddhist temples that same day? Let's do the math. She gave me *seven* numbers. So, of course, it took me *six* calls. But I did, in fact, end up getting a Zen Buddhist priest to agree to do part of Dad's service alongside a Presbyterian pastor and Bagpipe Mary. Because, when it comes to heaven and reincarnation or rebirth, we wanted to make sure we had all of our bases covered.

DO OVER:
Be helpful to others in the event of your unlikely, untimely demise. Keep the phone numbers of your doctor, your next of kin, pastor, and favorite Buddhist priest in your phone contacts. Not just the phone numbers of your favorite Chinese Restaurant and pizza place.

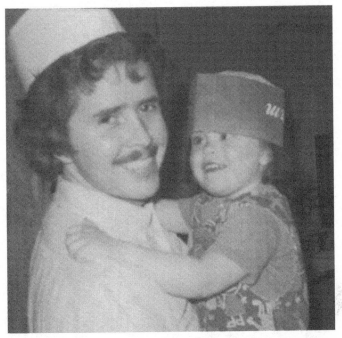

Dad and I (above). Imagine him with white hair and no mustache. He really did look like a Keebler Elf.

Hugs and kisses (right).

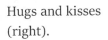

My dad walking me down the aisle June 21, 1992.

CHAPTER EIGHTEEN

SLOTH: IT'S A DEADLY SIN

When grief turns you into an annoying sloth: sometimes when grief begins to threaten to take you over, depression kicks in.

In all seriousness, if you need help with depression, or feel that you are in need of professional help, please flip to the Grief Resources section on page 205 for some websites, phone numbers and grief professionals that might prove helpful to you. But before depression kicks in, you may just become some version of a sloth. For me, this version of sloth involved lying on my side in bed, with lots of blinking going on.

ME: I can't move. Every muscle hurts right now. I may be paralyzed.

ALSO ME: But I can blink my eyes, so I must not be completely paralyzed.

ME: What if I've had a stroke and I just don't know it?

ALSO ME: I haven't had a stroke. I just have issues.

ME: Why can't I reach the television remote?

ALSO ME: Oh Gosh! Help! I can't reach the TV remote! Call someone!

ME AND ALSO ME [both yelling]: "Could someone please come in here and hand me the TV remote?"

Sloth: It prevents you from moving. It's also one of the seven deadly sins. It also annoys the *heck* out of the person who heard your panicked screams for help, and came running from outside only to hand you a TV remote that was less than four inches from your hand in the first place.

DO OVER:
In lieu of flowers, please send extra universal remote controls.

CHAPTER NINETEEN

THINKING ABOUT FAITH

If and when you reach a point when you need to think about what faith in God has to do with grief, read this.

I originally wrote this chapter nineteen months after my dad passed away. It took me almost two entire years to get to the point where I could write a chapter on faith. Faith is hard if you believe in a God that would never rob you of someone on purpose.

There are some truths that I have come to believe, and I hope they make sense to someone else struggling with their own faith in the aftermath of loss. Here's what I know for sure. I believe in a wonderful, big, merciful God who "knows every hair on our head." This is difficult to navigate because not only is it difficult to believe that God would let my dad leave us without so much as a goodbye, but it is even more difficult to face the person I have become. I am sometimes a crazy. Not crazy. *A crazy*. If I believe that God knows every hair on my head, how can I *also* believe that God can stand and bear witness to an otherwise sane girl who has not operated successfully on all cylinders for two years? Okay, readership, my sanity is only up for discussion for those who've seen the inner sanctum of crazy.

I like to believe, no matter how scripturally accurate or inaccurate I may be, that there is a special place for the followers of this amazing God. Never mind that part of the story when Moses doesn't actually make it to the Promised Land. Never mind that story of Jonah being a big sourpuss after he helped save the Ninevites. Never mind Job. I just feel sorry for that Job guy. And I definitely don't want to be *that* guy. Nobody wants to be *that* guy. Poor Job. Please don't let *that* be me.

I want to believe that faith doesn't make life easier but it makes life more manageable. If this statement is even the slightest bit true, I am so very afraid that my life is destined for some really difficult uphill battles with this giant God. If this is what God considers manageable, I'd like to review God's definition, and ask for a revision. Or a reprieve. Or time off for good behavior.

There are people who may believe that I should not question the authority of God. It has been my experience that, just like Jonah and Moses, when God really wants something to happen, God makes it happen. I have assumed, since the beginning of this part of my faith journey, crisis of faith, and/or adventures in grief that if God wanted to shut me up, God could at any moment throw me into the belly of a great fish. I think that would make for a pretty great, but even less believable story here in the state of Arkansas, where we are pretty landlocked. I expect that I am more destined to end in the belly of an unusually enormous armadillo or something that would be equally humiliating to have to tell one's friends about. I believe God loves us all. Believers and unbelievers. I believe even if you don't believe in God, that God believes in *you*. I believe that when God wants *you* to be an active participant in your own faith story, God can make that happen. It has become increasingly difficult to believe that a God who loves us so much could allow so much suffering in our world. While there are seven or so million readings on this subject, it is generally difficult for anyone to have proof. And so I trudge onward thinking about my faith, praying every day and hoping that someday this will all make sense in the Kingdom of God.

CHAPTER TWENTY

BRIDEZILLA MARATHONS

A short note on grief: dumb things grief makes you watch.

For one whole day of grieving, all I watched on television was a fourteen-hour Bridezilla marathon. Fourteen hours.

F-O-U-R-T-E-E-N.

Have you seen this show? It's something that the real me would never watch. It's the kind of reality show I loathe. It's a show about how horrible brides are to those who are trying to help plan the wedding, and the lengths to which the brides will stoop to get what they want. The brides on this show are portrayed as the most selfish, evil, cruel and impatient women our species has to offer. Whether it's real or fictionalized for television remains to be seen. The grooms on this show are portrayed as either the weakest men, or the most willing-to-go-along-with-the-program our species has to offer.

The "real" problems on this show are things like the dress was hemmed wrong. Or the cake wasn't adorned with the correct flowers or cake topper. Or the hairdresser messed up the bride's hair. Or the groom didn't do everything the bride wanted him to.

Or the bridesmaids, groomsmen, father of the bride, mother of the bride, and/or wedding guests didn't do everything the bride wanted them to. I think I watched the first episode, frankly, because I didn't have the resolve to make it off the couch to get the television remote control without crying. I watched the second and third episodes for the same reason that people drive slowly around traffic accidents: morbid fascination. I watched episodes four through fourteen because I really, *really* wanted one of the grooms to finally conclude how awful these women were, and for *just one* to see the writing on the wall and break up with their bride before it was too late.

I was astonished at what these women thought were real problems. Maybe it's because I have five kids. But....the hem of a dress? The wrong cake topper? Bad hair? Nobody doing what they're supposed to do? Most of these are problems that someone with five kids has before 6 a.m. on any given day.

Grief, and having five kids, does occasionally give you a better perspective. I was not a bridezilla. That's not modesty talking, that's the truth.

I'm not a bridezilla in any facet of life, and I don't like people who make crazy, mean or just plain unreasonable demands on their future or current significant others. I don't understand why any person would feel the need to treat another person that bad. I don't, and never will, believe that you have to be mean, controlling, demanding or demeaning to get what you want in life. Kindness and love over all else, right? *Not on Bridezillas.*

When I watched how these brides on the show treated those around them, especially (because of my perspective) their fathers, I was both sad and jealous at the same time. These women had their daddies standing next to them, supporting them financially and emotionally on what should be such a happy day in their lives, yet they were unappreciative and horrid to everyone around them.

If you were a bridezilla, or even if you weren't, and you still have your daddy, call him and tell him how much you love him.

If I could go back and do it again, I would tell my dad how much I loved him before he walked me down that aisle. And again at the reception. I wouldn't care if the hem of my dress was awful, or if the cake topper had trolls on it. I wouldn't care if they crazy glued my hair. Getting the chance to have one more moment of loveliness with my dad is what I'd wish if I could go back.

My money is on the fact that, as a part of Bridezilla episode number fifteen that day, the groom probably broke up with his awful, hideous-on-the-inside bride before the wedding. I never got the chance to find out. My husband walked into the room, took one look at me, removed the TV remote from my hand, turned off the television, and asked me to go get dressed.

Sometimes it's good to have someone who knows when you've turned the corner from normal grieving and are close to cracking, and makes you get up off the couch, get dressed, and go outside to breathe some fresh air. I still hope that last groom broke up with that bride. She was awful.

DO OVER:
For Real: Nobody should be that mean to everyone around them surrounding their wedding.

If I Knew A Real Bridezilla: I'd switch her cake topper so there were trolls or action figures. Nobody should take themselves (or a fancy cake) that seriously.

LESS THAN PRODUCTIVE WAYS I COPED WITH GRIEF

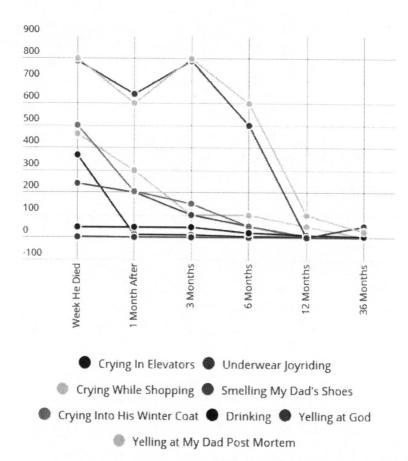

● Crying In Elevators ● Underwear Joyriding

● Crying While Shopping ● Smelling My Dad's Shoes

● Crying Into His Winter Coat ● Drinking ● Yelling at God

● Yelling at My Dad Post Mortem

It gets less awful. I promise. Sometimes with
the help of therapy and/or antidepressants.
Don't let this be you.

CHAPTER TWENTY-ONE

LAST WILL & TESTAMENT

If and when you are considering that" life is short" and you don't yet have a living will, or a last will and testament, read this.

Two days after my dad passed away, my husband and I went to Dad's apartment looking for answers. We entered his apartment and looked for papers or something that would indicate his wishes for a funeral, as well as for a burial. Or just for answers. And there it was – lying on a yellow note pad, lined up with file folders next to his bed. A note. A note to me. I don't think he intended it for me, but there it was, all the same.

The note read:

Wednesday to-do list: Get cookies, get paper towels, get toilet paper. And, underneath that, it read: "Write last will and testament."

And here's the moment in life when I finally figured out that irony is everywhere. Cruel irony.

Dear Dad,

I got the note you left me. Maybe you didn't leave it for me at all. Remember when you wrote on that piece of yellow legal paper next to your bed and scrawled the words "Wednesday to-do list?" And then you died on Tuesday? Remember that? Not very considerate, if you ask me. I'm sure it put a damper on your day as well. Grief makes me crack jokes. It's a coping mechanism that is horrifying to some. I apologize if you are in that group.

Well, there it was: the to-do list; right next to your bed, on the floor, just waiting for me to find it. So a piece of yellow paper made me cry. And, even more than making me cry, it left me both angry and sad (but mostly angry), wondering the following things: [These are all questions that I am now saving for my dad.] Dad – clear your schedule for a whole day when I get wherever you are.

1. Were you having chest pain since Monday, which made you add "write last will and testament" to the list? And – if so – how much chest pain would you have to be having to consider putting your last will and testament on your to-do list? On a scale of "ONE TO KEELED OVER DEAD" how much chest pain were you having? Because I want to know. **I need to know!**

2. Who scrawls "Write last will and testament," on their to-do list, **after** their grocery list? Who scrawls that at the bottom of the list? Who does that? It seems to me that writing your last will and testament should be slightly more pressing than bananas, toilet paper, and pretty much everything else at the supermarket. Maybe I'm wrong, but.....no. You **actually** died. So I know I'm right! That last will and testament thingy was the most pressing thing on the list.

3. Did you go to the grocery store right before you started feeling really terrible? Because at least having copious amounts of alcohol with the cookies and paper towels might have softened the blow. If not for YOU, at least for ME while I was in the process of finding and reading your list!

4. *And – even more so -what the bloody heck was on Monday's to-do list? What was so important that the last will and testament writing made the Wednesday list AFTER you got through whatever was on the Monday and Tuesday lists? Was Monday's list "buy ice cream, conquer the universe?" Or "buy batteries, help little old ladies cross the street, rescue kittens from trees?"*

5. *Why in the world was "write last will and testament" not on the MONDAY list?*

Maybe Monday's list was "ensure oldest daughter, who can't choose her own breakfast cereal, makes important end-of-life decisions for other people." If so, well played, Dad. Well played.

It is a fact that I can't choose between breakfast cereals. When I was a kid, it used to make you endlessly frustrated that a decision as simple as "Cheerios or Kix Cereal" would make me so nervous I'd almost have a panic attack. I also couldn't choose ice cream flavors. Or what to wear. But here's what you obviously needed to know, Dad. If you don't write anything down, if you don't finish your last will and testament (which you didn't), then I'll be your next of kin. I'll be the one making life and death choices for you. I'll be choosing for you. Based on what you "would have wanted." A lesser man might have thought that possible. A lesser man might have thought that sounded like a good idea. "Hi! My name is Heather Wallace, and today, I'll be making important choices for you because you forgot to write somebody better's name on your piece of yellow paper." Please Dad, please, consider writing somebody better's name on your piece of paper. If you don't, I'll most likely end up riding the crazy train around the block a few times. Or in therapy. Or writing a book about all of this. (Spoiler alert: all three) Please Dad, choose someone else.

Love, Heather

Someone should have told me all of this on Monday. If I only could have known on Monday what I know now, so I could get loaded on vodka beginning at 10 am Tuesday. Forget Italian food and sparkly shoes. I needed a stiff drink. I needed to be that one soccer mom doing recreational solitary drinking in her own kitchen that morning. It wouldn't have helped or improved my decision making process at all. But it would have softened the blow. Or at least given me a good reason for random vomit rising in my throat.

Grief stole everything from me that day, stripping me completely of my ability to decide absolutely anything. No one ever warns you that the time will come when you will be unable to choose. That the "choosing" part of your brain will refuse to work when faced with making awful, unhappy choices. Grief stole my choosing mechanism. I wasn't able to choose anything for about two weeks. My fourteen-year-old daughter helped me pick out my socks the next day and picked out my clothes for Dad's funeral. Thank goodness she didn't choose colored toe socks, which are her usual favorites. She chose for me, because I lost my own choosing ability. Someone else brought food for a while, so I didn't have to choose. Apparently part of my own "special brand of crazy" at this stage was "losing my ability to think in a reasonable fashion." I had a number of moments when I felt like my brain was submerged under water . . . going from racing too fast to too slow, causing a time delay in my thoughts and my actions.

Grief stole my choice. Until the only choice I had was to go on. Even when I didn't want to go on. I didn't want to go on without my dad. But I guess that's what surviving is all about; going on whether you make a conscious choice to do so or not.

DO OVER:
Write your own last will and testament today. Make your final wishes clear to those around you. Don't leave someone who will be permanently emotionally damaged in charge of your end-of-life choices.

CHAPTER TWENTY-TWO

DON'T BE AN ANNOYING CUDDLY BEAR

When grief turns you into a super annoying cuddly bear

Fact: I was not actually raised by wolves. Great, now this book will have to be shelved in the fiction section. Nor was I raised by koalas, however. To go from being a regular human among humans to a cuddly bear among humans is rough for other people to take. Sometimes when grief sneaks up on you with a baseball bat or machete, one becomes a cuddly bear. A super annoying, needy cuddly bear.

ME: *"Will you hug me?"*

MY HUBS: *"Really?"*

ME: *"Yes, really. Hug me again."*

HIM: *"Okay, but this is like the thirtieth time today."*

ME: *"But hug me."*

Note to self and others: This is probably only super annoying to others if it's completely out of character for you. If you are a natural-born hugger, this symptom may not apply.

HIM: *"Are you okay?"*

ME: *"Yes, but just hug me."*

Note to those who might entertain the notion that this cuddly bear "affliction" could be a good thing, because it might lead to random passionate . . . you couldn't be more wrong. Cuddly bear affliction does *not* lead to passion. It leads to sixty-seven repetitive verses of the "Hug Me, Hug Me Again" mantra, followed by a ridiculous number of hours of curling up in a fetal position on someone's lap, probably sucking your thumb.

Everything about cuddly bear affliction is annoying to those around you, so this is hardly a recipe for romance. And just when some of you *finally* thought maybe grief had some sort of silver lining . . . nope. Not unless the silver lining is that the hugging and whining goes away in less than a year.

People who are grieving need your love, unwavering support, and your nonjudgmental friendship. And your patience. It doesn't last forever. They are good people who have had something really bad happened. But the good is still there. And it will rise to the top. They need their friends, now more than ever. They don't need your advice. They need your love. They need your understanding. You don't need to say the right thing. You just need to wrap your arms around them and hug them. My prayer for each of you is that you don't have to have "been there" in order to have patience and compassion and love for your friends.

DO OVER:
There's no do over! What's wrong with hugging someone? Just keep the whining to a minimum.

CHAPTER TWENTY-THREE

SPLITTING YOUR PERSONALITY

If and when you think grief is splitting your one perfectly nice personality into two slightly psychotic and less than nice personalities, read this.

Do I even like ice cream? Did I before my dad died? Some days it's kind of rough to remember what my old personality even liked. Thanks to grief, there now seem to be two versions of me. The Old Me had the name my parents gave me: Heather. The New Me is named something else altogether, although I'm not sure what that name is. The New Me is someone I often don't recognize when I look into the mirror. The New Me doesn't like ice cream. That's only weird if you've known me forever. For the Old Me, ice cream comprised three of the four food groups. Maybe all four food groups, if chocolate chips could be their own separate food group.

I don't know if my distaste for ice cream is fueled by my dad's death combined with how much he loved ice cream. But since he died, ice cream just doesn't taste good anymore. My dad had a thing about ice cream. He always ate the good kind. He never had much money, but ice cream was the thing that he believed in splurging on. He always bought top shelf; never the yucky, grocery store generic brand that easily suffered freezer burn. There's a huge difference, if you're an ice cream connoisseur, which I think I used to be, before my dad died.

Now I can't stand the taste or the texture.

I tried to eat it in a bowl. No dice. I tried eating it out of the carton. Not any better. I slathered it with chocolate sauce and whipped cream. All I did was pick the whipped cream out and ate around the ice cream. So, clearly, something must be wrong with this ice cream in order to make me loathe it. It can't possibly be the not-that-gradual splitting of my personality. The New Me, the person I'm becoming, can't be crazy, right? I often find myself wondering what happened to the Old Me. Is she gone? I think the New Me has taken over.

Hey! You! New Version of Me! Yeah, YOU! What the heck is wrong with you? Why don't I like ice cream anymore?

The New Me is thinking more and more about a tattoo, which I've always thought was on my list of things I'd never ever do. The Old Me would need more liquor than is usually stocked in liquor stores just to get a tattoo, were she functioning on all cylinders. The jury is still out. I hate needles. Not in a "Hey, people, this isn't really my favorite thing," kind of way. More in a "I'd rather have my eyeball repeatedly stabbed with a fork with no medication than get any sort of an injection." I have this long held belief that most full-fledged, rational adults would have worked this I-hate-needles equation out long ago.

I have a young friend who is a diabetic. He regularly injects himself in front of me. Even after seeing him do it about a thousand times, I still get a choking and gagging sensation. Irrational Fears for five hundred dollars, Alex! So having a needle stab you repeatedly to make a picture on your skin has never sounded like a good idea. It has always sounded like an "avoid this like the plague" type of idea. And this "getting a tattoo" thing will be an experience to write home about, if it ever happens. Don't worry, I will have some sort of a lottery for those who want to go with me and see my response to that many needles (or that much liquid courage) in person; I promise an evening of absolute entertainment at my expense.

I plan to sell Groupons for this event.

My husband suggested we do a Groupon offering a Segway tour to the tattoo parlor, for all who'd like to be part of the audience of this spectacular event. With the number of adult beverages obviously required (for me), I'm not sure driving a Segway would be a good idea. Or getting body art.

My husband also suggested getting a company like Comcast to live stream my "Heather getting tatted up" event. He apparently believes I could get thousands of viewers, even more than a Pay Per View WWE Wrestlemania event. That's how badly he thinks I would behave. And I'm sure I'd be *super* classy, under those circumstances (I plan to blame this on the wolves who raised me).

Heaven knows someone, other than funeral parlors and the makers of urns, should be making money from unexpected grief attacks. There is obviously a market for neon signs advertising tattoo parlors across from your friendly neighborhood cemetery. In a perfect world, that neon sign should read "Grief Tattoos HERE," and "Half price if it's something you'll definitely regret later this month." I'm actually thankful there wasn't a tattoo parlor across from the cemetery where my dad's ashes are buried. Having "How dare you die without having the decency to say goodbye to me?" inked on my body would have been a financially and physically expensive mistake to make. And would take up most of my back, even in tiny font.

Another notable difference between the Old Me and the New Me is that the New Me is pretty decent at uphill running. My knee doesn't seem to mind anymore, even though I have a permanent knee injury. To be fair, I'm not sure that I can run hills all that well, all on my own. It might be more accurate to say that New Me is sometimes in such emotional pain that the knee is the least of my pain. At least three times lately when I've gone running, my iPod has run out of power halfway through the running process. The magic here is that the nanosecond that the iPod turns off, I can feel physical pain in places that I didn't know I had places. There are clearly nooks and crannies in my body that hurt after I run. Is it inappropriate to say that I have crannies? I'm uncertain, and trying to live my life aboveboard. The New Me is still somewhat inappropriate from time to time. When in doubt, always blame the split part of your personality to divert attention from yourself.

The lesson to be gleaned from this story is either:

1. Never leave your iPod uncharged so the music stops while you're running.
2. There is some possibility that your ears and your most painful body parts are somehow connected by grief.
3. Or possibly "Holy macaroni, stop running completely and just eat ice cream." You can tell by looking at me, no matter whether I'm masquerading as the Old Me or the New Me that, on my worst days, this phrase is probably my mantra.

Also, New Me is really bothered by any kind of language that is racially charged or ignorant. To be fair, Old Me felt this way too. But especially right now, anyone who uses the phrase "those people" in my presence is reserving themselves a very special place in the seventh circle of hell in my brain. Not to mention the words that refer to color, race, special needs or are just especially ignorant. There is more than a little irony in this particular paragraph because, since my dad died, my generic and ignorant cussing sometimes takes over at random intervals. Not completely uncontrollable hourly intervals, but regular intervals all the same. I don't think people need to swear at one another. I just don't. I think violent words breed violent behavior; this was something my dad taught me. In the whole time he was alive, I don't think I ever heard him swear more than once or twice.

I had a friend whose parents swore at her continuously. When I asked my dad about it once, he replied, "I don't swear at you guys because I don't think it ends the way people hope it will. I treat you better than that, and I expect you to treat others better than that." I still think about that. It brings so much irony and guilt because, since his death, sometimes I get frustrated in a way I never have before. And I do, in fact, curse. Sometimes at people. I didn't do this before his death. I think mounting frustration has definitely added to my new identity as a random user of cuss words. So I suppose I have a little something the new me can work on. Because feeling like you're certifiably crazy three-quarters of the time is *obviously* not enough for the new me to be working on. Eliminating the gratuitous bad language should be on the short list as well.

New Me wears dresses much more frequently than Old Me ever did. And high heels. I think New Me looks good in high heels. And most other people think so, too. I'm not sure this is the worst problem in the world. At least now I get out of my pink sweatpants and go to work. For about two weeks after my dad's death I was worried that I might, instead, consider the life of a homebound kitty cat hoarder. Reminiscent of the Old Me, I still like to buy Disney bandages. Today I'm wearing a Disney "Cars" bandage to hide the blisters on my feet. But still....all high heels, all the time.

New Me has random and sometimes hilarious crying episodes at the most inopportune times. Old Me wasn't much of a crier, but New Me is definitely an off-kilter, teary-eyed, emotional mess. More than once I've had to assure strangers that I'm not in need of men in little white coats to take me away. It's both funny and sad, and good to know, I guess, that people at the grocery store get really weirded out when someone in a cocktail dress has an uncontrollable bout of crying while holding a head of lettuce. It's also funny and sad that there are video cameras throughout the church I work at. I just hope nobody is watching those tapes.

I think this random crying stint version of grief is extremely special and delightful when it happens in the airport, at department stores, or in the elevator of random office buildings. People are really scared of lunatics. Especially one that, on first glance, doesn't appear to look like an ax-murderer but could be, because of her publicly erratic behavior. It's always the ones you don't expect who turn out to be ax-murderers, right? In Arkansas, whether you're a lunatic or not, they're also expecting you to most likely be packing heat. So if seemingly without provocation you start crying at random, in front of complete strangers at any of these locations, people begin to laugh nervously while slowly and cautiously edging away from you.

Apparently this particular version of New Me is prone to panic-inducing uncontrollable sobbing. It's *super fun* for everyone involved: the crier, and the people pondering whether the crier is an ax-murderer. And, by *super fun*, I mean humiliating and horrifying to all parties involved! It's even more awkward when it takes place in an elevator where people cannot move or look away from you. It's virtually impossible for them to get away from you (at least very far away) if you're in an elevator. There's nowhere for them to go between floors. It's a great social norms experiment that I highly recommend to those who are excessively bored with their lives. Nothing says "I'm probably an unlikely looking Lizzy Borden" quite like gasping, choking, and full-out sobbing seemingly without provocation in an elevator full of random strangers who are trying to figure out how they will escape if you *do* decide to commit mass murder. I suggest if you do this, just for fun consider adding in my extra-special touch: wiping your nose on your sleeve. Nothing says "get us the HECK out of here" quite like strangers who are watching you lose your mind while using your sleeve to keep snot from running down your dress.

I'm so glad I'm already married. Without the benefit of being married, this whole year would have been a recipe for prospective dating suicide. People like to talk. Out there in the real world, a big crying mess who scares people in elevators could never get a date. I don't care what E-Harmony or FarmersOnly.com says.

I think the part of split personality my dad would have liked is that I can see the new version of myself starting to fight for the things that I want most, which I might not have fought for as the old me. Before he passed away, Dad and I had a few conversations about how there are things in life that you can't always just wait around for. If you want to go back to school, have more kids, have more friends, change your relationships, write a book, change jobs or careers, or find things that make you happy, you shouldn't just drag around and hope that life will happen to you. Because someday you'll be too old to go to the dojo, or you'll lose your binocular vision. I don't worry much about losing my binocular vision. Snot running down my face, I do worry about.

I will always regret one thing. Dad told me he really wanted to move far away, somewhere warm. I gave him the sour grapes and two thumbs down. Old Me didn't pitch a fit very often with my dad; that Heather didn't usually do that. In fact, almost never. This time I did, because I didn't want him to move away from me and his grandchildren. I pitched a huge fit, complete with full-on adult crying and heaping enough guilt on him to convince him to stay in the area where I lived. So we could spend more time together. That certainly didn't end the way I thought it would. I think I should have let him go. He would much rather have gone out, heart attack and all, on a warm, sunny beach than on a city street in the freezing cold Midwest. I blame myself a whole lot. I think letting him fly south would have meant warmer weather. And maybe warmer weather would have prolonged his life. Most of all, I think I should have let him go because everyone deserves to be happy. And if that means turning your life upside down, even if it's only for the sake of a new adventure, I don't think anyone should stand in your way.

I'm sorry I didn't get the chance to tell him that. New Me seems to understand Dad's need for adventure, everyone's need for adventure, more than Old Me ever could. Maybe that's one awful regret the old Heather had to experience to become the new and maybe improved Heather. I think New Me heard enough of my dad's stories to know that he had times when he felt like a victim of circumstance, when he really should *not* have been. And to learn that I don't ever want to fall victim to circumstance, because I can choose many things which happen in my life. And, for the things I can't, I can choose how I respond to those things. I am learning that I am so much more than just "what happens to me in life."

New Me seems a little clearer on the whole "you should do whatever you have to do to be the best person you can be, and to choose happiness for yourself." New Me seems to have a much better, more intentional handle on what I'd like to spend the number of heartbeats I have left doing, and who I'd like to spend them with. Although, to be fair, there are people whom I love with all my heart who were scared off by the grieving process, and how crazy it made me. I would love to have those people back in my life. Grief does have the power to be a relationship killer.

Right now, I'm trying my best to be some compromise/merger of my old self and the new me. The person who doesn't like ice cream very much, but sometimes likes chocolate pudding. Who doesn't just let life happen, but tries hard to say and do the right thing in the right moments. The person who isn't a victim of circumstance, but who understands what it is to be the hero of her own story. The person who is nice, even when she's geeky and wiping her nose on her sleeve and tripping down the stairs in her high heels. And I'm trying. I am trying. I promise.

It seems the more I try to forget who I was before, what I've been through, and the things I don't want to feel, the more they make themselves known. The new me doesn't seem to want to forget the old me, but wants to fold her into the new person I am becoming. For now, I'm going to try to be a little kinder to myself and not fight the merger of Old and New Me. Because I'm pretty sure that's a losing battle. I'm going to allow myself to grieve when I need to, feel when I need to, allow myself to love people I want to love, and to see emotion as a *good* thing, without being so hard on myself. I'm going to try to just be me, and let some semblance of the merger take place. And maybe that's the best anyone can do.

DO OVER:
Try not to scare random strangers (or family and friends) with out of the blue, uncontrollable bouts of crying in elevators. Take the stairs.

POSSIBLE SELECTION CRITERIA
FOR YOUR NEXT OF KIN

A Helpful Guide
Can the person you're choosing
do the following things?

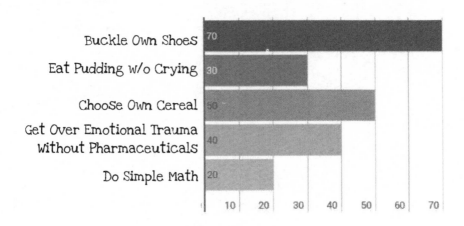

Buckle Own Shoes — 70
Eat Pudding w/o Crying — 30
Choose Own Cereal — 50
Get Over Emotional Trauma Without Pharmaceuticals — 40
Do Simple Math — 20

CHAPTER TWENTY-FOUR

DON'T GOOGLE YOUR SYMPTOMS

When grief turns you into the person who believes they have every disease ever chronicled on WebMD.

In fairness to myself, when someone you love dies, mortality becomes very real. And when someone you love dies suddenly from an illness or an ailment, grief can lead you to believe that you are next. Paranoia. It's a *thing*. It's *real*.

ME: My stomach hurts. And my chest hurts. I think I'm dying.

ALSO ME: I'm not dying. I'm just being crazy. Or paranoid. Or both.

ME: I really don't feel well. I'm just going to google my symptoms.

ALSO ME: Don't do that. It never ends well. You've just been crying all day. That's enough to make anyone feel a little sick.

ME: Nope. Nope! It says right here . . . it's not just the crying. Stomachache, headache . . . I have typhoid. I definitely have typhoid!

ALSO ME: You do *not* have typhoid.

ME: Read it! Read the symptoms!

ALSO ME: You don't even *have* any of these symptoms.

ME: I have flu-like symptoms. Gimme back the computer. I'll tell you what I have.

ALSO ME: Sigh. I am officially crazy.

ME: You're right. I don't have typhoid. I have hemorrhagic fever.

ALSO ME: Is that even a real *thing*?

ME: Yes, it says right here. Flu-like symptoms. It's almost identical to Ebola. I'm dying. I'm *definitely* dying.

ALSO ME: It also says you get it from being bitten by a bat. Have you recently been bitten by a bat?

ME: What if I've been bitten by a bat and I didn't even know it? My dad had a massive heart attack and didn't know it. I could definitely have been bitten by a bat and not even know it.

ALSO ME IN A PANIC: *Dave! I'm on Web MD and I think I might have been bitten by a bat. And now I have some form of Ebola.*

MY HUSBAND: *Let's go get you a milkshake. Put your computer away.*

DO OVER:
Anytime you feel like googling your symptoms, whether you're dealing with grief or not, don't. Just don't. Call your doctor, or drink a milkshake.

CHAPTER TWENTY-FIVE

TRUE CONFESSIONS

On the day that grief makes you re-evaluate your opinion of yourself, read this.

Confession: I really miss my dad today. But not his karate stories. Today was full of heartbreak. I find myself clinging to some new, extremely sad reality as I am starting to forget what his voice sounded like. Sometimes when I close my eyes, I think that when I open them, maybe he'll be standing right here. But I know that I am fooling myself, and it's not going to happen.

Today my family started bringing Dad's stuff to our church rummage sale, which is a game all in itself. The rummage sale is the most exhausting of our youth fundraisers. For the next week, it will keep me tethered to church for about fourteen hours each day, including the weekends. But it's just business, right?

It's just business. Because I'm certainly not going to open any boxes full of my dad's things that will make me wonder where the heck he is. And why he doesn't show up and, at the very least, unpack his own stuff. Is there a sarcasm font? Reality check. Choke back tears. *Pull yourself together, new version of me!*

In the last month or two, I have been very clear on who I am and who I think I was meant to be. Here's what I'm learning about myself. I'm learning that, sometimes with very little warning, I'm an emotional train wreck. Not in a little-engine-that-could way. More like I've-been-derailed-and-am-most-likely-going-to-crash-into-a-building. I hope this train derailing is not permanent. And, I promise you, so do the people around me.

I'm learning that I miss my dad, and I use both theater and bad jokes to cover it. If I could get a paying job that would incorporate these two things, that would be a great situation right now. Unfortunately, I'm not sure Saturday Night Live needs a writer who goes from hilarity to excruciatingly hard sobbing while curled in a fetal position in the corner. Although that might make for an excellent character.

I'm learning that I like to make jokes about my dad being dead. Making jokes is:

a. Not good manners
b. Not seen by others as extremely classy
c. Hard for other people to take
d. My obvious coping mechanism
e. A tactic that doesn't hide the pain, but covers it like a bandage over a bullet wound
f. All of the above

Answer = F.

I've decided that I primarily make jokes about my dad being dead because I figure if Dad was here, he'd never take this kind of back talk from me. So sometimes I hope he'll show up just like Jacob Marley in *A Christmas Carol* and tell me that the chain I'm forging in life is going to send me straight to you-know-where. Or to wherever the bad Buddhists go. His coming back, even for a moment, would at least give me one more opportunity to look pompous and annoyed while I have to listen to all of his stupid karate stories. It's the "I dare you to do something to stop me" tactic of dealing with your real life problems. Dare the person to come back and bring the behavior you're exhibiting to a screeching halt.

I am learning that I have been a big jerk. Please refer to the portion where I reference having to listen to his *stupid* karate stories. If I ever learn lessons I needed to the first time, the second time, or even the fifth time around in every facet of my life, maybe today wouldn't be so painful. A few years ago, if you had the audacity to tell me that I'd miss those *stupid* karate stories about winning medals against men half his age, the same stories over and over, I would have laughed in your face. I'm most definitely not laughing now. Irony: I miss the stories. Like crazy.

I am learning that I am good at cutting bulletin board letters. I learned that you turn the paper, not the scissors, people. Or like Lindsay, one of my best friends, you can just get a Cricut machine and let the machine cut your letters in half the time it takes to do it manually. This has absolutely nothing to do with my dad. But in the grand scheme of things, if you're making a list of things you're still good at after grief strips your life bare, even cutting bulletin board letters seems like some sort of an *amazing* triumph.

I am learning that I am marginally good at pouring coffee with a smile. Another incredible talent that's just so marketable in the real world. But important to remember when you feel like saying, "Grief has stolen my life. I have nothing left." I have something left. It's coffee pouring, but it's something. Coffee, anyone?

I am learning that when I wear high heels, more people talk to me. I blame this on the fact that I am almost five foot three, in three or four inch heels. I'm not sure why more people like to talk to me when I wear heels. Maybe "I wear heels" and "I mean business" are in some way synonymous. Frankly, I'm quite sure the people at the grocery store can only see me over the deli counter when I'm wearing heels. I am definitely going to try to wear crazy seven-or-so-inch high heels to the grocery store and do a social norms experiment of some kind. Maybe go to the store early in the day in my pink sweatpants and sneakers and go back later all dressed up in heels, and see how people treat me differently. People shouldn't treat you differently based on your high heels. This also has very little to do with my dad, except that grief makes you feel like you look terrible every single day. In wanting to feel better, I sometimes want to look better. I don't always want to feel like I'm fading into the woodwork. So I wear heels. It sometimes makes me feel better, even though it won't bring my dad back.

I'm learning that grief affects my weight. For a while, I wasn't eating at all. Some days I eat all the time. It's like being pregnant, only without the happy little bundle of joy to look forward to and to blame the weight on. People treat me differently based on how much I weigh. This is an ugly fact of life that I hate. And when I wear something nice and I know someone is treating me a certain way because of how I look, I hold it against them. On the other hand, the few people who have loved me at ninety pounds and at one hundred and ninety pounds, and every weight in between, have a special place in my life and in my heart. When I began to realize that a few people were always there to answer their phones, to sit with me, to hold my hand, to really speak into my life through the grieving process, I realized that these people were the people who I should give my heart to for my whole life. They don't see just the ugliness and tears; they see the real me. Everyone should have a few of these people in their lives. I'll loan you one or two of my people if you need a good start.

I am learning that at least right now, I make no sense to anyone, least of all me! I'm not sure that's just a stage of grief, but I think I used to be at least fairly predictable, if only to myself. So I'm hoping this is just a stage. I'd try to argue that I'm still fairly predictable, but you've recently read a chapter about me joyriding in my unmentionables, so we all know that would be a *big lie* right now. I'm not so sure if predictability comes and goes with grief, or *when* my ability to make sense to myself will return. I have high hopes that grief has only temporarily stolen my predictability, but I'm still trying to get this part of grief figured out.

I am learning that I pray only for miracles for other people. Maybe for someone who has always tried to be a very faithful, albeit mixed up Christ follower, it is acceptable to get mad at God and to stop praying for miracles in your own life because of grief. I like to think God grants miracles whether I refuse to ask for my own or not. I asked for a miracle the night of my dad's death. For the theologians in the group, I know bargaining with God is not a good, theologically savvy thing to do. In any case, God said no to my miracle. I don't really care *why* God said no. It's difficult to pray for your own miracles when you've been turned down for the *big* one. It's not just that I despise rejection. It's that I really want my dad back, and I'm ridiculously angry about not getting the miracle I prayed for. Ridiculously angry at God.

While grieving, I learned that I am easily frustrated by things. And that there are stupid and random things that make me cry. But in order be able to handle the balance of life and keep the status quo, I've allowed only two people on the list of "private individuals who are allowed to make me cry" at any one time. So if today's not your day, good for both of us! This is an interesting quandary if you are the mother of five children, all who have the ability to make you cry with a simple "I love you" or a "Mom, I know it is midnight, but I have a research paper that I haven't started and a puppet show about asparagus, both due tomorrow. Do we have any poster board? Can you help me make some puppets?" I am learning that I can only handle five problems at a time. Again, maybe today's not your day and you're off the hook! Right now I handle these five problems like a flight attendant: two exits up front, two waves of the finger to the back of the plane, and one in the middle. Not that finger, people. I have slightly better manners than that. Also, I have decided to use the "conquer and destroy" method of problem solving. When that doesn't work, I do the "consume a small trough of chocolate pudding and then cry because you'll never again be a size six" method. I feel that, while none of these are the answer, it will get easier to find more ways to cope as I go along. It strikes me that I may need a whole lesson on coping skills.

GRIEF TIMELINE

1 YEAR AFTER MY DAD'S DEATH

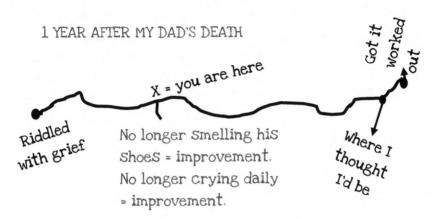

Got it worked out

X = you are here

Riddled with grief

No longer smelling his shoes = improvement.
No longer crying daily = improvement.

Where I thought I'd be

18 MONTHS AFTER HIS DEATH

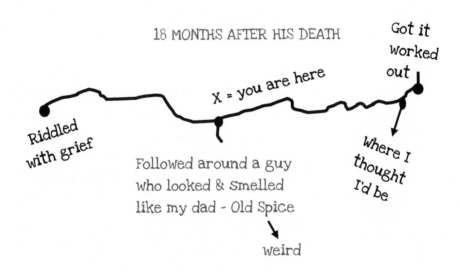

Got it worked out

X = you are here

Riddled with grief

Followed around a guy who looked & smelled like my dad - Old Spice

weird

Where I thought I'd be

CHAPTER TWENTY-SIX

URN JEWELRY: JUST ANOTHER PHRASE I WISH I'D NEVER HEARD

On the days that people try to sell you funeral, legacy, or remembrance knick-knacks, read this.

A few weeks after my dad's death, bereavement ads began to show up in my mailbox. And in my email. I'm not sure how the Google algorithms work on the internet, but apparently when you Google in random succession things like flower arrangements, funeral homes, Buddhist monks, and bagpipers, something in the recesses of your computer that has to do with selling stuff to the bereaved begins to hop up and down gleefully, clapping its virtual hands and yelling stuff.

"Yep! Put them on the list! Someone died! They're in the market! Maybe a tombstone is in order! Maybe they'd like a Groupon for a hearse ride around the big city!"

That's how I imagine it happens anyway.

I somehow ended up on a remembrance mailing list. Computer algorithms are amazing, but the number of things that people can track or know about you, based on what you google, is a little scary even for someone who doesn't much care if *Big Brother* is watching. Rather clearly, however, since I never received mail like this before, I ended up on some sort of list for the bereaved. They knew someone in my life had died and they were sending me ads and order forms to purchase urn jewelry.

I don't think the words *urn* and *jewelry* belong in the same sentence, in the same way that I don't think the words *lingerie* and *joyriding* belong in the same sentence. Some of these ads spin it differently, calling it "cremation jewelry" or "memorial jewelry." None of this fancy spin-doctoring words change my negative feelings about these things, unfortunately.

It's jewelry with your loved one's ashes in it. And, since the crematorium lost my dad's body for some length of time, I'm not sure that I could ever be completely convinced that we received his actual ashes. I try not to think about what might really have been in that box.

When the first mailing came to our house, I immediately threw it away. But I was intrigued by the thought so, against my better judgment, I googled it so that I could find out more later. It turns out that urn jewelry isn't just for people; you can also have your pets cremated and keep their ashes. This part was the hardest to take. Did you know that you can make a print of your dog's nose, and they will make a necklace out of it? Fun fact! I live to teach people things they never wanted to know.

I know there are real stages of grief that seem to be recognized by some medical professionals, and then there are stages of grief that I've made up to fit my own story. As part of processing grief, I recommend you keep a journal and write down your own stages. Anger is a real stage, both recognized by professionals and recognized by me.

When I began receiving literature on urn jewelry, I was still very angry; not just because Dad had been ripped away from me, but also *at* my dad because I like to play the "what if" game with

132

myself. This, by the way, is most certainly *not* something I've found to be a particularly helpful game to play when one is grieving. I was angry at my dad because I will always wonder what would have happened if he had gone to the hospital first thing in the morning, instead of waiting a good twelve hours trying to "tough it out." His heart attack, in some format, had gone on all day. That much we know. While considering all these "what ifs" in my head, if someone had handed me a necklace with his ashes in it, I fear the rather rapid downhill spiral of crazy may have taken me to the point of no return.

All I know for sure is if I had been wearing my dad's ashes on a chain around my neck or inside a ring those first few weeks, everyone I know would have encountered some measure of getting to see me express this anger and random "let's give Dad the serious-no-holds-barred talking to that he so richly deserves." Nobody wants to see someone yelling at jewelry. It's weird.

I've been a whole bucket of crazy these past four years. Grief took me to some places that I could never have previously imagined. I can say with complete honesty, however, that had I been wearing Dad's ashes around my neck those first few months, I would have been forever known as the girl who randomly talks to, and cusses at, her necklace in the grocery store. I was not happy with my dad, and I would have let him know it.

There is another side to this. I know people who wear urn jewelry or keep their loved one's ashes in their living room, because it makes them feel like they still have a piece of that person. For those who need that to help heal, I would never "yuck your yum." *You do you.*

The ridiculous side to this is that had *I* been the recipient of urn jewelry, I would probably still be slamming my urn jewelry down on counters while talking to it. And probably not all that nicely. The more serious side to this is that there are so many important lessons that grief has taught me. And one of them is that once you've lived through grief of your own, you should never judge the grieving process of another person. No matter how much they talk to jewelry. For other people, having an urn or memorial jewelry might be the thing that gets them through their lowest point. If that jewelry makes them feel closer to someone they've lost, that will never be mine to judge. Every person needs to get through grief in their own way, in their own time. If having a ring with your dad's ashes puts you in a place when you no longer cry into bowls of chocolate pudding, then you should always wear that ring. Please, for the love of Pete, *always wear that ring*!

For almost four years I have struggled with the goodbye I never got to say. And will never get to say. And so I held on to possessions and memories of my dad. For months after his death, I was still smelling his shoes. Feel free to judge; I am comfortable with the crazy I've been. I'm going to come back stronger, and hopefully without the need to smell people's shoes. Let's face it, even if you're crazy and you miss someone so much your heart is breaking, smelling their shoes is still weird. The first stage is admitting it, right?

I am now almost on year four, and I can finally talk about my dad. And write about him. Without crying. Most of the time. I don't need to curl up in his jacket as much as I did those first few months, because it does get less awful. I gave away his shoes because I needed to stop being the weird kid who smells people's shoes. I might still be the weird kid; it's just not because of shoe smelling anymore. It took me what seemed like an excruciatingly long time to arrive at the conclusion that I don't need urn jewelry because my dad is still everywhere for me. I see him in the eyes of my children, I hear his laughter in my own, I hear the things he used to say in the things that my younger brother says to his own children. I see his face in the faces of my three brothers and my two sisters and in some of the features of my own children. I carry him with me. But not in a necklace. In my heart. And that's even better.

CHAPTER TWENTY-SEVEN

SHUNNING OF THE GRIEVERS

On the day that your friends start to break up with you,
read this.

It seems so very strange that, while writing about the death of my dad has felt completely impossible at times, this chapter has still proven to be one of the hardest chapters to write. In navigating the past four years, I have clung to the people closest to me. I have hung on so very tightly because I have desperately needed to believe that life is ultimately good and beautiful and still full of wonder, even when one is fighting a daily battle with sadness and loss. I have not at all been myself. I have often been a person whom I hardly recognize when I look in the mirror. I have taken so much more than I have given, especially from those who are closest to my heart.

One of my biggest struggles with grief continues to be that I am not completely ready to move on and let my dad go. And yet, even though I know that this particular fact is somewhere in the minds of those who surround me with their love, they are ready to move on, even if I'm not. My struggle is not necessarily *their* struggle. I do not know how long it will take me to move on, or if I will *ever* completely move on. When I began this journey, I thought that grief was like a bad cold, or the flu; you have it for a period of a few weeks, but then – just like that – it disappears. When I began this journey, I thought grief was like getting a cut on your arm or leg; you apply antibiotic cream, cover it with a bandage, and within a week or two you peel back the bandage to find it has healed.

I found out that I was wrong. So wrong. Grief is not like a cold, or like the flu, or a small cut on your arm or leg. Grief leaves a scar. Sometimes multiple scars. It doesn't disappear as suddenly as it appeared. It is my fondest hope for myself and for others that the grieving process will continue to prepare all of us to be better in the future; to be more loving, caring, compassionate, and more patient with those whose struggles may last even longer than mine has.

But in the midst of all of this grief, the people around me have gotten tired. People don't always have time for your brand of crazy when they have their own crazy lives to deal with. In the midst of all this grief, what I needed most was a group of people I could cling to tightly and not let go of. People who were my rocks, my anchors, and my lighthouses lighting my way back from my own personal darkness. I have needed the people who have loved me forever to say that they will love me no matter how grief changes me. It has been my fervent prayer that the person I am becoming can still be loved by those closest to me. I am not the same as I was before losing my dad. *Not at all.*

For better or worse, the people I have always been closest to are people who hold their own personal details and struggles – and mine – close to their hearts. People who would never reveal my darkest secrets. People who love me no matter what. And who know that I love them no matter what happens, no matter where I am, no matter what I say, no matter where our lives take us.

In the last year, I have come close to losing at least one, if not multiple friends. Maybe I've actually lost one or two. Okay, so I have lost one or two. People who say things like, "If they were really your friend, they would still be here," are sadly mistaken. I am no longer a child, and neither are my friends. It really isn't that simple. Nobody really knows what grief can do to a relationship until they've lived it. And even after they've lived it, grief is different for everyone. Grief manages to take your worst fears, the most glaring faults in your personality, and the things you struggle with the most in life, and magnify them all by one thousand, and then lay them out for the whole world to see. You find yourself in situations when all you truly want is for someone to hold you and say that you are going to be okay. You find yourself in situations when you need every person in your circle to tell you they still love you, even when you are unrecognizable to yourself.

My husband is a great man. One of the best I'll ever meet in my whole life, I'm quite sure. He is one of the great loves of my life, and he is a blessing from God that I could never deserve, no matter how much I try to be perfect. He is an amazing, faithful, patient, loving partner versus my own crazy, impatient, stubborn, perfectionist persona. He is a ridiculously awesome, calm, collected and loving father to our five kids. But he is not the only person who is a lifeline for me, and he knows it. And vice versa. I was born into a family with five other siblings. And sometimes I go to them both with good news and bad news, before I go to my husband. I was also blessed with a childhood that did not go exactly as planned (did I mention I was raised by wolves?), and an adult life that did not go exactly as planned. As a result, there are a handful of people from both stages of my life that have all become the loves of my life – a statement that I will absolutely never apologize for.

When my dad died, I sent a few of texts. One went to my husband. The others to people who are, have been, and always will be, some of the loves of my life. They are often my heart, my soul and my lifelines. They carry my heart in the palms of their hands.

I have worked for a church my whole adult life. My faith is absolutely the guiding light in all of my relationships, but I know that there are people who cannot and will never understand that for me, the love of a lifetime isn't reserved for one person. The love I have for my siblings, my children, and my friends is very much the "love of a lifetime." Not everyone can understand my friendships (and probably my choices as well). For better or worse, I've known since I was a kid that I might not always be able to explain the unconditional love I have for those closest to me. This was about the time when I met some of the people who hold me the closest. I cannot always explain it, nor can I make those who haven't experienced that kind of love understand it. I have learned to take it as it is; I have been given a gift from God in the unconditional love of a team of people who have largely been with me more than half my life, and that particular gift is not mine to challenge. And I wouldn't change that for the world.

Without a shadow of a doubt I know I am a difficult, but I hope sometimes worthwhile, friend to have. I am stubborn and short tempered. Grief has sometimes heightened those things. I am not usually needy but for the last three or so years, I have absolutely been needy. The neediest. I have needed to cling to all of the loves of my life – my husband, my children, my siblings, and my friends. And for my friends who are in primary relationships with other people, some of their significant others have learned to love me and understand me. But others, not so much.

I'm going to try to blame this on grief. Grief sometimes makes people whom you really love, and who really love you, want to break up with you as a friend. I do need to qualify this by saying that grief hasn't made me lose my grip on reality completely. I am in touch with reality enough to know that if you hang on too tightly, if you need more from someone than they are able to give, even if they *are* one of the loves of your life, you risk losing them. And grief didn't do that. Needy behavior (in this case, *my* behavior) did that.

Not having someone who has been the love of your life, or a lifeline or friend, in your daily life becomes a secondary loss. In my mind, a secondary loss is just as painful as the original loss. Sometimes even more so. It's one thing not to be able to hold onto someone who has passed away, and *another thing altogether* to struggle to hold onto people who are still living.

For me, grief began because I lost my dad. And because I was not good at battling grief on my own or with the resources I had on hand. I needed everyone around me to rally the troops and be on my team. I sometimes still need the people who hold my heart in the palm of their hands to reassure me that I am going to make it through. That I am not going to fall apart. That I will be stronger on the other side.

Unfortunately, things don't always go as planned. *Otherwise I would have had no need to write a book about grief.*

For those who've managed to hang on through this process with me, some because you live with me and can't get away, I am forever grateful. I promise I will continue to take steps to get better and to shake as much of the grief from my life as I can. And for those who've had to jump ship because of circumstances, because life is hard, or because they've had their own garbage to deal with, I want you to know that grief, in this form, doesn't last forever. You don't stop being the love in another person's life because of struggles in the past, present, or future.

I believe with my whole heart that God puts people in our path for a reason. The people who become the loves of your life cannot be swept off the path by the side effects of grieving. People spend their entire lives trying to create and working toward building loving friendships and relationships with one another. They have to try. In some cases, they have to try hard. I have been blessed enough in my life to have a few of these forever friendships thrown in my life, and in my lap when I was very young, without even trying. The gifts of friendship that God has given me are my treasures on earth.

Grief cannot steal those treasures. Grief can only try one's patience. But much like Moses in the desert, patience is not always rewarded in the next ten minutes. Patience and friendship and the loves of all of our lives are rewards that last a lifetime.

It is my hope that grief – in this format – does not last a lifetime.

Grief cannot shatter the love of the people who have always held you in the palm of their hands.

Love is much more permanent than grief and in the end, I'm pretty sure love wins.

At least, that's what I'm hoping.

DO OVER:
1. Love those around you unconditionally.
2. Love people through grief, if they are the griever.
3. Grief is hard on relationships. Don't give up on your friends even if they don't know how to love you through grief.
4. Love will eventually win. Grief won't. Hang on tight. It's a bumpy ride.

CHAPTER TWENTY-EIGHT

SOME FAITH IS CHOCOLATE, SOME IS VANILLA

If you cannot completely relate to the grief of a wigged out soccer mom who has lost a parent, but you've lost a sibling, a child, a friend, or someone else in your life, please read this.

I know not everyone can or will experience grief the same way I do. Thank goodness! As a part of this process, I have had some really funny moments (maybe only in retrospect) and some really awful moments, which I would never wish on my worst enemy. There have been some dark moments. And, on one of my darker days, our church pastor invited me to a new ministry called Faith & Grief. This ministry completely changed me for the better, especially when I needed it the most. For more information about the Faith & Grief ministry, visit www.faithandgrief.org.

The Faith & Grief ministry hosts a luncheon once a month at churches around the United States, including our church. It is a luncheon for grievers, giving us time to share our stories in small groups, eat together, pray together, read scriptures, and listen to a speaker who shares their experience with grief and how it is shaping their faith. This ministry has brought me such a long way from where I was. It is such a relief to meet with others who are also grieving, and to have a safe place to make some progress on my thoughts about grief each month. It helps to see that I am not alone in my struggle with grief. It helps me to see people in very different stages of grief, to be able to see a little glimpse of how far I've come, and it gives me glimpses of how I can use my grief to help others in the future. I strongly believe that every community needs their own Faith & Grief ministry. Please see my author page for contact information if your church would like to start their own Faith & Grief group. I'd love to answer your questions! As always, God never gently and tenderly places people on my path. I love that image, but I just don't think that's part of my life story. I am the girl who God shoots out of a cannon so that I can land with an explosion, or a fall from the sky, or an embarrassing fall down a flight of stairs, which all make for a grand entrance, right? But God does this always in the right place, with the right people, at the right time. These Faith & Grief luncheons were no exception. I have met so many amazing, wonderful, compassionate, loving and caring people through Faith & Grief. I have gotten to really know some members of our congregation that I would not otherwise know except in passing, as well as some members of our community. And, well, God always seats one unsuspecting fool right next to the biggest weirdo God can find. That's me. When God is looking for a weirdo, I try my best to oblige. I make weird look easy.

And so, from day one, God seated this really nice guy, who is the father of one of my youth group kids, at my Faith & Grief luncheon table. This youth group dad also happens to be in the Air Force. So between the uniform he wears to the luncheons and the plain old weirdo that I usually am, our table is known as the "fun table." We might be the only two people who actually think that, to be fair to the other tables. In any case, for the past year Lieutenant Colonel Stuart Rubio, otherwise known as Stu, has been sitting at my Faith & Grief table, tolerating my stories about chocolate pudding and my dad. There's a special place in heaven for Stu, and all of the other people who've sat at my table. But especially for Stu. Because I think while it takes one stone cold weirdo to recognize another one, he actually agreed to share parts of his journey through the loss of his younger brother not only with me, but as a part of this book.

Somewhere in the middle of writing about my own dad, I realized that not everyone would be able to relate to the way I process or deal with grief. As previously mentioned, I'm not always as forward thinking as I'd like everyone to believe. Grief has many different flavors; most of them not nearly as pleasant or as uncomplicated as chocolate or vanilla. I'm pretty sure my grief is more like Rocky Road. But as far as processing my own loss, I am a girly-girl. I like dress up clothes, tiaras, tutus, and peach roses. I have processed my grief through embarrassing stories that involve lingerie, public emotional outbursts, and trying out every type of waterproof mascara on the market. What I wanted, more than anything, was someone who processed grief differently than me. Someone who was a guy's guy, who would be willing to collaborate on this project, and wouldn't be caught dead joyriding in lingerie or sobbing in a parking lot. Although you might find him sobbing when his team, the Nebraska Cornhuskers, lose.

Through the Faith & Grief luncheons at our church, I had the opportunity to listen to Stu's story. For those who process grief more like Stu, we both wanted to be able to share his story. We hope some people who are experiencing grief and can't do it through the eyes of a girly-girl will find Stu's story relatable in different ways than mine.

Conversation number one.

ME: *I know you process practically everything about grief differently than I do.*

HIM: *Are you referring to the fact that I don't actually own lingerie?*

ME: *Very funny, and I'm sure all of our readers, your wife, and your family will be ridiculously relieved to hear that. Especially since I just called you a "guy's guy."*

HIM: *Is this the part where I have to be honest and say that I do wear cycling shorts regularly? [He's a triathlete.]*

ME: *You're a guys' guy. Even having to say the word lingerie out loud in front of me practically makes you squirm. So quit messing with me and just tell me what the worst part of grief is for you right now.*

HIM: *Aaaahhh....it's all hard right now. But I think the music is, by far, the worst part.*

ME: *The music?*

HIM: *You know what I mean.*

ME: *No, I really don't.*

HIM: *There are songs I just can't listen to anymore because they remind me of Jamie.*

ME: *Songs you can't listen to? Like what?*

HIM: *Well, there's "Hate Me" by Blue October. And then there's "It's So Hard to Say Goodbye to Yesterday" by Boyz II Men. And then there's "The Peace Carol" by John Denver and The Muppets.*

ME: *It strikes me as a little strange that you'd be thinking about listening to those three songs together on a playlist for any reason, not solely based on grief.*

HIM: *Before you go on about things that are strange, did I happen to mention that only one of us doesn't own lingerie or think about drinking shampoo that she thinks smells like bacon?*

Me: *Touché. So there are songs you can't listen to, because they're too painful?*

HIM: *Don't you have songs you can't listen to because they make you think of your dad?*

ME: *Only the Bee Gees. I hate the Bee Gees, through no fault of their own. Do you have any others?*

HIM: *"Empty Chairs and Empty Tables" from Les Misérables.*

ME: [Trying to process how all these things fit together on one playlist – I'm sure my mouth was gaping open, and I was trying not to laugh.]

HIM: *Shut up.*

ME: [Regaining my composure] *Okay, okay......so give me some songs you can listen to because they don't trigger grief or make you think of Jamie.*

HIM: *I've basically limited myself to metal and hard core rap because I can't handle anything else. Is this for the book?*

ME: *Yes. So give me an example I can use.*

HIM: *Well, I have a few songs that don't fit into either one of these categories and don't make me think of Jamie...but the songs in these categories are really awesome.*

ME: *Like what? Gimme a good one.*

HIM: *Rihanna's "Bit$% Betta Have My Money."*

ME: *Never mind. You're killing me.*

Conversation number two.

HIM: *I visited Jamie at the cemetery this afternoon. I hadn't been back there since the funeral so I'd never seen his headstone in person. It was very painful...I hadn't cried that much in a while.*

ME: *I'm so sorry. I've done that a couple of times, but the first time is definitely the worst. It does get less awful. I don't know if this will help you, but it has helped me to know that my dad's not really where his headstone is. The headstone is a painful reminder, but for the next couple days, if that bad pain in your chest is still there, try to think about all the places Jamie probably really is. I don't know which of your kids looks or acts like him, but I'm betting one of them does and I'm betting you can see him in one of them.*

HIM: *Well, at least one of them has his competitive spirit and participates in lots of the same sports Jamie liked to play with me.*

ME: *It has helped me when I've gone to my dad's grave to think about something he would have liked. Or even think about or plan to do something with my family that I did with him when I was a kid. It makes me sad, but it's also a reminder of the happy places where he really is. My dad's in my heart and Jamie's in your heart. He's not in the ground. He's with you. I promise you that's the truth because there's no way a guys' guy like you would agree to regularly eat croissants and fruit cups* [a staple at our Faith & Grief luncheons] *with someone who regularly describes herself as the real-life version of a cross between Fozzie Bear and Scooby Doo. Especially if you couldn't tell that my grief was getting better, based on the support I get at these luncheons, and if you didn't think this group was helping you too.*

HIM: *I do like croissants.*

ME: *I'm glad that's what you got out of my previous diatribe. And if none of the "focusing on the good times" works, I have tons of lingerie you can borrow.*

HIM: *Thanks, but no thanks.*

ME: *Do something this week that Jamie would have loved. Hopefully that will help, and hopefully that won't involve you needing to borrow my lingerie for any reason.*

HIM: *God help us both if that happens.*

Confession: Our Faith & Grief group at church is a little bit of a come as you are party. And because this is the way (my) life works, I usually dress like a youth director. So unless I am dressed up for meetings that day, I sometimes show up in jeans and a shirt. But Stu Rubio doesn't. For the past year while attending monthly Faith & Grief luncheons, he has come directly from an Air Force base to our group lunch. And he isn't wearing jeans and a T-shirt. He's wearing this thing that he calls a "onesie." I've been assured by his wife, Megan, that it's actually called a flight suit.

And that phrase "everyone loves a man in uniform" is real, in case you were wondering. It's real. It's not a myth or a meaningless phrase. It's a thing. People stop him in our church parking lot and thank him for his service. People come running up to stop him on his way into Faith & Grief luncheons to shake his hand and give him a hug. People love Stu Rubio. They love Stu Rubio not *just* in an "I'm a Lieutenant Colonel in the Air Force" kind of way. They love him in an "I'm a cross between Batman, The Flash and Superman" kind of way.

Since I've seen his playlist and, after you've read this book, you'll have seen part of it as well, I know that he's also a regular person. Although there's not much that's regular about him. Except that grief levels the playing field.

If you've read this far and haven't yet figured out that I'm definitely not the super hero type, perhaps you need to re-read the chapter on lingerie or review the part where it took me the better part of two weeks to change out of my pink sweatpants. One of the very best things about our Faith & Grief luncheons is that they are "lightning strikes" kind of people: individuals who might not necessarily have that much in common but are brought together by grief. Although I'd much rather be brought together by a really stellar ice cream social, if given the choice. So, when the soccer mom version of Fozzie Bear from The Muppets ends up sitting next to Batman/The Flash at lunch, it's a really strange combination.

Faith & Grief luncheons are the same meal each month. We always have a box lunch that includes a croissant sandwich, a fruit cup, and one cookie. And because Stu knows that I think people treat him like Batman, which he doesn't see at all, he likes to use that to make jokes that make me mad.

Conversation number three.

HIM: *Is your fruit cup warm? Because my fruit cup is warm.*

ME: *Is it supposed to be warm? No! Mine's not warm. Mine's cold. Why is yours warm? Is everyone's warm except mine? Did you get a special fruit cup? Are you the only one who got a special one?*

HIM: *My fruit cup is warm. It's no big deal.*

ME: *It's a big deal if you get special treatment because you're Batman and I'm Fozzie Bear.*

HIM: *Hey, wait....did you get something from the mini-bar when you came in? [We have a no liquor policy at the church] No? Maybe that was just me. I can't believe you didn't get anything from the mini-bar. Maybe they just missed you.*

ME: [Fuming]

HIM: *So I suppose this is the completely the wrong time to ask you if they also gave you a hot towel on the way in?*

ME: *I hate you.*

HIM: *Wait! How many cookies are in your box lunch? [There is always only one.]*

ME: *Do you think there's ever been a fist fight at a Faith and Grief luncheon, or will today be the first one?*

HIM: *Okay, Okay. I'll stop. I'm done. I promise. How many packets of mayo did you get?*

ME: *Tell me when you're finished.*

HIM: [Laughter]

It's terrible being friends with Batman.

CHAPTER TWENTY-NINE

JAMIE'S STORY

I first met Heather about six months after I lost my twenty-seven year old brother, Jamie, in a car accident. He was the older of my two brothers on my dad's side of my family, and eleven years younger than me. Of my four brothers, Jamie and I had the most in common. We were both active in sports, enjoyed the performing arts, and both followed our favorite sports teams with a sometimes unhealthy passion. But Jamie outshined me with his natural compassion and drive to serve others.

We both loved cycling and running, and I had always hoped that one day I could get Jamie to share my love of triathlons. At five years old, he competed in a short-distance bike/run event for kids that was held right after one of my triathlons. Jamie was the only one out there on training wheels, but was determined to compete and finish. In what we would learn was typical Jamie fashion, when he received his participation medal, his initial reaction was to feel sad because he won a medal and I didn't. He was very perceptive and caring, especially for a five year old!

Ten years later, Jamie and I were on a week-long bicycle ride across Iowa together, and there were portions of the ride where we were riding alone on the road, just the two of us. On that ride, Jamie shared his future goals with me. As an adult, he wanted to continue the mission work he had been exposed to with his church youth group, and also wanted to become a doctor and join Doctors Without Borders. He was fifteen years old...seriously! When I was fifteen, all I worried about was football and how to talk to girls. I was twenty-six at the time of that ride, and I was *still* mainly just worrying about football and how to talk to girls.

In the years before his death, Jamie had been struggling to find a direction. He was two classes away from earning his degree in psychology from the University of Nebraska with nearly a 4.0 grade point average. He had been pre-admitted into multiple very competitive Master's programs across the country. But for some reason, Jamie just lost momentum and quit school. He continued working as a counselor at a home for wayward boys, something he was exceptional at. The boys he worked with really looked up to him in a different way than the other counselors. Jamie was the only counselor the boys loved enough to work together as a team and bake a cake for his birthday. They also begged the home to take them to his gravesite after his death, despite the hour-long drive.

But Jamie struggled in other areas. I'm not talking about substance abuse, just bad relationships and bad financial decisions. The crux of both of these problems seemed to link back to the fact that he cared so much about people, and gave so much of himself to his relationships. In fact, I strongly believe that the reason he remained in a relationship with the woman who was ultimately responsible for his death had everything to do with the calling he felt to care for her two children. He acted as their parent, taking them to events, like their school orientation night, when she just didn't care.

Our age difference and similar interests drove a relationship where Jamie looked up to me. This became an issue when Jamie began to get off track. In the last few years of his life, Jamie pulled away from me because, in my mind, he didn't want his choices to disappoint me. This led to long periods of time when we didn't communicate at all. I reached out to him on occasion but, in looking back, it could have been much more often. That caused a pain that I have yet to overcome. I wish I could tell you I've reached the point where I accept that I did my best, but I'm not there yet. But as I travel on this journey, I've been constantly reminded (by family and close friends) to trust that God is leading me through the valley and will eventually return me to higher ground.

Stu Rubio with brother Jamie (2010).

You may need to seek professional help for grief if theoretically speaking (or for real) you can't stop crying over the following:

CHAPTER THIRTY

UNHEALTHY OBSESSIONS

Since Jamie's passing, I've worked hard to keep his spirit close to me. Luckily, we shared so many interests that just doing the things I normally do keeps Jamie with me every day. Of course, I now approach some of these shared interests with a much more intense devotion. Or, as Heather calls it, an unhealthy obsession.

Last year, I didn't just train for, and compete in, a few local triathlons as had been my pattern for many years. Instead, I hired a coach, trained at a whole new level, and enjoyed unprecedented success (for me) in my races. I thought of Jamie every single time I was out running or spending hours on my bike. When I had to endure Jamie's first birthday after he died, I started the day with a long run and went faster than I thought I could possibly go that day. And just before the one-year anniversary of his death, I returned to race at the same site where Jamie had originally helped me to the finish line. I envisioned him running with me, not just across the finish line of that particular race, but every finish line of every race I ran, the very same way he did once when he was alive.

While many members of my family are talented music makers (as I once was), I've resigned myself to a life of simply appreciating music made by others. I listen to music in the car, while working out, doing household chores, and occasionally at work. Here's the problem: While dealing with grief, certain songs seem to take on a whole new meaning. Songs that remind you of the person you lost become too hard to listen to. Songs that make you think, "Oh I bet [fill in your loved one's name] would love this song," become off limits. Songs that you heard any time in the days after their death are added to your "Do Not Listen" list. In addition, intentionally sad songs become *totally unbearable!* Even those sappy eighties and nineties hairband ballads are impossible to listen to. "Every Rose Has (*absolutely does NOT have*) Its Thorn" is on my playlist! And, yes, it's even worse than the CD I couldn't listen to for years after breaking up with a college girlfriend.

So, I've created some charts that outline some of the songs I cannot listen to, because they make my sorrow worse. I'm sure lots of people who are experiencing grief also have a list. Following that is a playlist of songs that I can listen to, because these songs don't trigger episodes of grief. Most of the songs on my "CAN Listen To" playlist (some of which Heather made me "bleep" words out of so this book can continue to be rated PG-13) contain language not appropriate to use in front of your grandmother and content inappropriate for nine year old children. If you're looking for songs appropriate for your grandmother or your nine year old, I recommend you stay far away from my "these are the songs I can listen to" playlist and instead buy Grandma and your nine year old a song off of Heather's playlist...like "Free To Be, You and Me."

The World According to Lieutenant Colonel Stuart Rubio.
Songs he can't listen to because they add to his grief:

"I've basically limited myself to metal and hardcore rap because
I can't handle anything else (not a joke)." -Stu Rubio

"No way is he listening to any of these songs right now."
-Heather Wallace

It's So Hard to Say Goodbye to Yesterday   -BOYZ II MEN
Hate Me   -BLUE OCTOBER
The Peace Carol   -JOHN DENVER & THE MUPPETS
Iris   -LIVE
I'll Be Home for Christmas   -CROSBY
Empty Chairs At Empty Tables   -LES MIS
My Immortal   -EVANESCENCE
Christmas Song   -DAVE MATTHEWS

The World According to Lieutenant Colonel Stuart Rubio.
Songs he CAN listen to because they don't add to his grief:

ON STU'S PLAYLIST

B@$#% Better Have My Money
-RIHANNA

Bring the Noise
-ANTHRAX & PUBLIC ENEMY

Insane in the Brain
-CYPRESS HILL

All I do is Win
-DJ KHALED

Can I Get A....
-JAY Z

ALSO ON HIS PLAYLIST

Sexy And I Know It
-LMFAO

Turn Down For What
-LIL JOHN

Can't Hold Us
-MACKLEMORE/RYAN LEWIS

I Will Be Heard
-HATEBREED

Tik Tok.
-KE$SHA

In addition to the songs I can and cannot listen to, I've also had a few conversations with Heather about one other "unhealthy obsession." In this case, I'm talking about the love for the Nebraska Cornhuskers football team that Jamie and I shared. As native Nebraskans, we were both dubbed Nebraska fans at birth. I grew up following the team with my dad and quickly brought Jamie into the fold as soon as he was old enough to wear red. We stressed, we screamed, we cried, we danced, we high-fived, and we talked about the past, present, and future of the team for hours on end. It's something that sports fans of many different teams have experienced and shared with loved ones. I can't really say that I've immersed myself in the Huskers *more* since Jamie's death, because *I'm not even sure that's humanly possible*. But I have cherished it more and am enjoying passing this on to my sons. And, while they haven't reached the point of obsession (like Jamie and I), they proudly wear their Husker gear and cheer for the team with me (or quietly slip out of the room to avoid my wrath if the game's not going well). I've also been known to drag my wife and the boys along to games that they may not have chosen to go to on their own...mainly because the weather conditions made Hoth (Star Wars reference) look like a top Spring Break destination!

So, my obsession with the Nebraska Cornhuskers has only heightened since Jamie's passing. The Husker traditions (and Jamie's spirit) live on through our family, and I share this obsession with my wife and sons. If you and your loved one shared an interest, sometimes throwing yourself into that interest after they've passed away is a good thing, and sometimes not so much. Only YOU can decide if your grief is lessened by continuing to do whatever it is you used to do together. If it brings you joy through grief, by all means....obsess away!

I've included some pictures of our family's obsession with the Huskers (and each other) throughout the years.

Stu and his dad, Rob Rubio, braving the cold and rain during a game against Colorado (1996).

Stu and his brothers, Jamie and David, getting fired up for their annual winter football game...a tradition Stu and his dad started when Stu was seven (1995).

Stu's then fiancée, Megan, and dad take Jamie to the ground in another annual family football game (1997).

Stu, Jamie and their dad celebrate Nebraska's third national title in four years at the intersection of 72nd and Dodge in Omaha (1997).

Stu, his dad, brothers Jamie and David, wife Megan, and sons Ashton and Ethan celebrate an exciting overtime win over Iowa State. (2005)

Stu with his dad, Jamie, and Megan enjoy each other's company but not this game against Texas A&M. (2007)

Stu and his dad before a game against Northwestern. (2013)

Stu and his three sons, Ashton, Ethan, and Evan, before a (below) freezing game at Penn State. (2013)

Stu, Megan, and Ashton, before yet another below freezing game. This time against Iowa. (2015)

Stu and his oldest son Ashton hanging out with Herbie Husker. (2015)

CHAPTER THIRTY-ONE

BACK TO HEATHER

If you are drowning, clinging desperately to anything or anyone familiar read this.

The one commonality Stu and I have had throughout the grieving process is what we fondly call "unhealthy obsessions." When grief steps into your life, it's easy for unhealthy obsessions to creep in. And being a sports nut isn't one of the unhealthiest obsessions, in the grand scheme of things. Lots of people are obsessed with sports and it has *nothing* to do with grieving. But grief is a time when seriously unhealthy obsessions such as addictions to alcohol, drugs, porn, computer games, and a host of other things, as well as neediness, clingy-ness and anything that helps dull the pain or helps you hold on to your loved one creeps in. In Stu's case, I think hanging onto to the football team that he and Jamie both loved has helped Stu process some of his grief. In my case, I became consumed with something I'll refer to as desperately drowning.

As far as this book goes, I had a ridiculous amount of inner struggle as to whether to include this chapter. In the end, the need to tell this story won out over the humbling sacrifice it took to write it. Mainly because I don't think I am, have been, or will be the only person who goes through this part of the grieving process. Even though it really hurts, I am telling this story with the hope that it will not hurt anyone else in the process. And because I believe so very strongly that the truth will set us all free. And also because if you are out there somewhere, and this is part of your story, you need to know that there are people who survive grief. The aftermath of grief does not last forever. There is another side that you can reach after the ugliness of grief releases you.

Before grief stepped in and tried to ruin my whole life, and did a pretty fair job, I had a friend. He was someone who, no matter how far we lived from one another, or where time or space had taken us, had always been close to "best friend" status in my life. This is a friend from my childhood who had been my lifeline through many of the very best and worst moments of my life. He is one of the loves of my life. For the purpose of this story, we'll call him Samuel, because in the Bible the story of Samuel being given "back to God" when he was a child, fulfilling the promise his mother Hannah made to God, and then Samuel conveying the message of God to Eli, the priest in the temple, often reminds me of this person. For me, my own real-life Samuel had been the promise God sent me time and time again. He had not only been my lifeline, but he was often the answered prayer when I cried out to God in desperation. Samuel had been the quiet voice in my life that told me I was going to be okay, even when I did not, or could not, believe it for myself. He had been my encouragement and was often the crazy glue that put me back together when I wouldn't let anyone else even get close enough to see how far gone I was.

I will answer the question that is about six seconds away from being asked: I am not the kind of girl who would ever have an affair of any kind. I think I better qualify this by including a waiver clause: *I reserve the right to amend this statement if I ever have another psychotic break.* Especially one that begins with me thinking I'm wearing clothing when I'm actually driving in broad daylight in my lingerie. Just kidding.

Did I ever date Samuel? Yes. For about seven and a half seconds in high school. Are we married to each other? No. We are both married to other people. For my part, I have been married to one of the greatest, most loving and compassionate people you could ever meet. A husband who loves me with his whole heart, and who makes my heart sing and has made me laugh until I cry for the past twenty-four years. I may have inadvertently told you how old I am, if the Bee Gees reference didn't already blow it for me. For my husband's part, he already knows every single part of this story. He has lived this grief with me. And I can tell every one of you that there are really, *really* horrible ways in which life teaches you about who loves you unconditionally, and grief is one of the meaner, uglier ones. For my whole life, I have considered myself the luckiest girl because I have found out, in some cases the hard way, that there are people who *do* love me unconditionally. My husband is one. Samuel was another, for most of my life.

Right after my dad passed away, I began the process of desperately drowning. There are people who will step forward and, not that helpfully, suggest that if you have problems, emotional, mental, and otherwise, you should tell only your spouse. However, I would like to believe that not many would dare to judge this situation. Especially if they were desperately drowning while moving across the country and trying to raise five kids, all at the same time. It doesn't have anything to do with faith, or the Bible, or whatever view you have of Biblical marriage. It has everything to do with the process of desperately drowning. If you are married and one of you is drowning, it goes without saying that the other one has to take care of the kids. And the house. And the dogs.

If you are drowning and you are married, your spouse has to make sure you, the drowning victim, is fully clothed, not in pink sweatpants, and that you continue to go to work because you need your paycheck because your kids still really, *really* like to eat.

During times of desperately drowning, you might reach out to people who aren't living your grief and who aren't trying to raise your kids at the same time. In the months following my dad's death, I had moments when I couldn't bear to pray at all. I also had moments when I prayed like a crazy maniac for days on end. For the record, there is a difference between praying without ceasing, and praying like a crazy maniac. I'm pretty sure only *one* of them includes simultaneously dancing to Atlantic Starr songs, and refusing to get out of your pink sweatpants. Even surrounded by all of the lovely, happy kids I work with and their parents and their friends, I have never felt so utterly alone and deserted by everyone including God, at times. I was angry. I was sad. I did not want to talk to or listen to God. But I will always listen to my Samuel. And I think God probably knew that.

Samuel, the kid next door from my childhood who always answered his phone when I called, had already built enough credibility in my life for me to trust and listen to him. He is one of only a few from my childhood who earned the right to "speak into" my life, even when I'm messing it up. Every single day, Samuel assured me on the phone that I could make it through, that he knew I could make it through. He may have been lying through his teeth on some of the worst days. Once, on the sketchiest, scariest days, he offered to get on a plane if he had to, if it was a matter of life and death for me. Samuel would not let me die, nor run away from my life, which was a definite possibility, especially in the middle of depression. Samuel has often been the kind of friend I aspire to be. Almost every phone conversation was met with tears (mine, not his); the tears of a person who has regret, and will never get to say goodbye to her dad, the tears of a person who doesn't have the perfect life, the tears of some combination of the fifteen year old that I was when we met and the forty-something that I am now. On the other end of that phone was this voice – this person I have almost always known who has enough issues of his own to have every reason to just hang up. Instead, he just listened, and knew when to repeat over and over, "It's going to be okay."

I had lost my own ability to see that things were going to be okay. Rather Biblically, I could not carry my own cross anymore.

Lucky for me, God sent someone who would act as my Simon of Cyrene – although more willingly, because Samuel had known me so long. Just as I have done for him a few times, although perhaps not on this level.

I want you to know that if you are desperately drowning, there will be people who will stand extremely close to you, mostly just to keep you alive. Because they're *that* worried about you and, in my case, they were right to be. Further, there will always be people who cannot understand that kind of closeness. There is a portion of the population that believes that if you are "that close" to someone, especially someone of the opposite sex, there *must* be some sort of a sordid (I love that word) affair going on. They are led to believe that even if you are not having a physical affair, you must certainly be having some sort of an emotional affair.

For those who have never been desperately drowning, I offer what I've learned. I'm quite sure there are, in fact, people who do have affairs, who stray from their marriage, or whose marriage doesn't work out. If you believe your spouse is cheating, maybe that's true. Whether they are or not, if you *think* they are, I suggest you consider counseling. Because marriage requires trust. And somewhere in the space of when you fell madly in love with your spouse and when you started to think they were cheating, that trust has somehow been damaged or lost, and needs help in order for your relationship to survive. If, however, you believe your spouse might be having an affair with someone who is desperately drowning, *please* give him or her the benefit of the doubt. Because they very well may not be having an affair; they might just be helping someone else hold their head above water.

Don't get me wrong. Someone who is desperately drowning in grief is most definitely in a bad, sad, scared, and lost enough place to be an easy mark for someone who wants nothing more than a sexual affair. I didn't include emotional affair here because, at least in my case, grief stripped me of my ability to be much more than a pathetic-feeling, sobbing puddle most of the time. When grief takes over and you feel as if you've lost everything, it can present an opportunity for a really manipulative, sleazy creep with the worst intentions to act like your friend. He or she might swoop in and present oneself as a hero, and look like someone you might want to sleep with, and perhaps you do. However, if you're reading this book, it's my best guess that you want to learn more about grief, or you want to feel less crazy standing next to my personal brand of psycho. Or you're the kind of person who wants to understand the power grief really does have over people. And this chapter is about the *unbelievable* power grief can hold over a person.

I decided to write this chapter even though my mother, along with others who suppose me to be a reasonable, upstanding, moral human being, might read it. Which, in my case, may cause my mother to tell people I was probably raised by wolves and certainly not by her.

I need those who are grieving to know they could be an easy target for moments of weakness that include affairs and addictions of all kinds. But, even more than that, I need absolutely everyone to know that if someone loves you unconditionally and you are desperately drowning, they will continue to stand by your side, no matter how temporarily crazy you become. And they would never exploit your weaknesses at your worst moments.

I was raised with a good girl mentality, and don't like to think about affairs or other things that seem like a whole lot of effort with no positive or productive results. I guess I believe it is possible for someone who is desperately drowning to have an extra-marital affair. There is certainly a hole in your heart that is so deep that most people who've been there would try almost anything to fill it. Grief definitely has the power to make you do things you never before even considered as a possibility.

But that is definitely not my story. In my story, I'm still not sure what the ending looks like, but I live my life being accountable to my own conscience and to what I think God wants for my life. And because relationships in real life are so very fragile, my Samuel found himself in an absolutely impossible situation. He was trapped between his wife, the girl he married and loves with his whole heart and the life they built together, and his childhood friend whom he had known most of his life, and who was really suffering in the aftermath of losing her dad and herself in the process. Samuel and I did not have an affair, but his wife was concerned about the status of our relationship. Although I really don't know her, I'm sure she is a lovely person. But she's dead wrong about her husband and, quite obviously, she doesn't know the first thing about me. In the only sentence that I would ever dream to write that could speak for both Samuel and I, we would never have an affair with each other. Not ever. Even the wolves that raised me taught better. I have much more faith and respect for myself, for Samuel, for all of our children, and for my spouse to ever be that kind of girl. While I am fully aware that there are people who wrongfully judge others and put them in the affair category, largely because I'm not sure most people can understand unconditional love without some sexual component, I left this chapter in for two very important reasons.

First, I want people who are *not* grieving to understand how destructive grief can be. And, similar to mental illness, to not be afraid to have difficult conversations about how it can affect one's life. Anyone who has ever spent four and a half seconds with me would burst out laughing if you called me a homewrecker. But I do want people to know that grief became a cancer in my life for a while. I am in no way, shape or form a homewrecker. And I did not, and would not, have an affair. But I was suffering and that suffering caused me to be ridiculously needy and hold on to Samuel with all of my might. I have always trusted him, and I needed him to really step up and be the best friend he's been to me through many parts of my life. I needed him to say the right thing. I needed him to be there and to listen. I needed him to be on the other end of that phone while I often cried my eyes out. The loss of my father made me look at absolutely every relationship in my life and want to scream at the top of my lungs, "Please, please, please....don't you leave me too!"

If someone you love is acting as a support person for someone they care about who is desperately drowning, I absolutely implore you to go with what you *know* about that support person. Please do not go for what society says as far as "what it looks like."

Here's what I want you to know. While you were busy not trusting your spouse, he was busy keeping a terrible secret: He knew someone who was desperately drowning, and every part of her life was being ripped apart piece by piece. If I had been diagnosed with cancer instead of grief and depression, and was talking to my support person on the phone or crying into his ear while going through chemo and losing my hair, would society have judged those moments as probably having an affair? I doubt it. The very same support provided to someone with a life-threatening illness would not be seen as something seedy. The real truth is this that grief often goes untreated because, just like serial killers, a grief-stricken person looks just like everyone else.

Second, I want the bereaved to know that sometimes you will find yourself desperately drowning, and you will want to latch on to anything or anyone that comes your way. Be sure to choose your friends during this time very carefully. And stay away from addictive substances and activities. And seek professional help right away if you have even a hint that you might need it. I have often called myself the luckiest girl. If you've read this far, you already know that phrase is only ninety-nine percent true, unless I consider crying into chocolate pudding something that is "lucky."

I will tell you, however, that lots of things went wrong while I was desperately drowning, and did not seem that lucky, the least of which was that my best friend's wife thought we were having an affair. For the record, I am still the luckiest girl. Chocolate pudding, lingerie, crying episodes and all. I am the luckiest girl. My husband took care of our house, our kids, our dogs, and listened to me during the worst moments of my life. Samuel continually answered his phone during the worst time of my life, and listened to my tears, my fears, and my crazy I-no-longer-belong-on-this-planet-with-other-humans behavior. The truth to be gleaned here is this: Could we have had an affair? Not likely. By not likely, I mean that it is possible in the realm of real life. But only if Samuel was a sleazy creep that wanted to take advantage of my wigged-out weakness. And only if both of us were less moral people. And only if the desperate drowning left me wanting to fill that empty hole in my heart with more ruin and destruction (what fun!). And only if I didn't genuinely believe that Samuel was destined to be one of the best friends I'll ever have, and if he wasn't also convinced that was true. Would we have had an affair? Absolutely, unequivocally no. He is a person who definitely isn't a sleazy creep, we both have some pretty unwavering moral compasses, and some big dreams for our futures. Independently of each other.

Thankfully I never reached a point when grief stole my moral compass enough to consider sleeping with someone who wasn't my husband. As much as Samuel has loved me since we were kids, I guarantee that he would have done everything humanly possible to prevent me from causing further ruin or destruction to my life. Because he knows that the real me, minus grief, loves him (as well as a whole bunch of other people), but I love my husband more. And differently. Samuel knows what both of those loves look like, and he's not particularly confused or dazzled by where that line is drawn. It's beside the point, but I want to point out that Samuel has seen me in a gold sweat suit, so let's just say that any "I'm trying to impress you" factor ended in about 1988.

Did we have an affair? No. I've never had an affair. But I would never judge someone who has. Because every person on this planet has walked a different path, and I don't really know where all of those paths lead. But I'll tell you that mine led right back to God. I am still the luckiest girl, and this is why. The very first day I met Samuel, I was fifteen years old. He had dated a girl who had a less than great reputation, and gossipy people liked to talk about her and the less than stellar things she'd done. Before I met Samuel, I passed him in the hallway at school as he stood with a group of friends talking about this girl with the bad rep. High school is sometimes ugly and brutal, but it can also change your life if you are in the right place at the right time, which is what knowing Samuel has taught me. His friends continued to have terrible things to say about this poor girl and, as I passed by, I heard him stop them. He stood up to his friends and defended the reputation of a girl whom he was no longer dating. He defended the reputation of someone because it was the right thing to do. From day one, Samuel has been that guy who stands up for what he believes, no matter what it costs him.

I used to believe that some things in life were simply coincidence. I used to believe in chance meetings, in things that just seemed to fit perfectly together without explanation, and in strange moments when life just seemed to be leading me in certain directions. There are things that I used to believe were coincidence that I now attribute to the Holy Spirit working in my life.

So you see, I left this chapter in because for me it represents a secondary loss. I am not currently anywhere in the life of someone whom I love, who I know loves me. I am no longer in Samuel's life because of grief. Being needy led to a misperception by others that we were something other than what we've always been, and that is thick as thieves. For Samuel, there should be no shame or blame in this situation. His biggest crime was no crime at all. He stood by the side of someone who was desperately drowning, and held that person (me) close to his heart. He also refused to tell the secrets of both the really dark place I was in, and the really terrible things I was going through. Sadly, because relationships can sometimes be fragile, misperceptions took hold. And in my fractured condition, I could no longer hold my own against accusations that Samuel and I were something that we definitely were not.

The broken pieces of me and the shattered pieces of him, after fighting so hard and continually hurting each other as we tried to figure out how to remedy the mixed up opinions of others, finally gave way to a situation of complete surrender on both our parts. We surrendered most of our friendship to the delusions of other people, and to the opinions of those who don't even matter, and of some who do. I am still the luckiest girl in the world because my husband has heard every single story about my life, has lived through grief with me. During all of the desperately drowning moments, my husband knew that I needed someone in addition to the person raising my kids and dogs, a friend who had known me forever who would be there for me. My husband knew I needed additional backup, and trusted that it wouldn't replace our marriage. I truly am a person who believes that love is something you should share with everyone you can, everywhere you can, for as long as you can. I believe that love isn't like a bucket of water; you don't run out if you use too much. Because there's really no such thing as too much love. My husband knows that grief threw me into a proverbial lake of fire, and that everything I touched for the better part of three and a half years disintegrated right in front of me. But, for better or worse, he stood next to me. And so did my childhood friend, Samuel.

I am the luckiest girl in the world because, since I was fifteen years old, I have had this wonderful man (his name is not really Samuel) in my life who is one of my heroes, although he'd be the first to tell you he doesn't think he's much of a hero. Since I was fifteen years old, we've exchanged phone calls and visits and often been the "fixer" for the other one, that one friend who can straighten the other out when one of us is in serious distress, or about to be seriously stupid. Since I was fifteen years old, I've had a friend who has loved me unconditionally, even when I sometimes didn't deserve that love, which really is the definition of unconditional love.

I am the luckiest girl because since I was twenty years old, I have been married to a different man who has seen me through the best and the worst, but who is well aware that he is not the only person in my life who I love unconditionally. Best of all, he welcomes my friends, our children, my family, our church family, and my youth group kids with open arms into our home and into our hearts. He doesn't have a jealous bone in his body, and lets me just be me. I am the luckiest girl in the world because, while I was still so very young, God put both of these amazing men in my path, for different purposes and to play very different roles in my life. Because perception often gets the best of people, I often very deeply feel the loss of my friendship with Samuel. And I feel completely heartbroken over this loss. He hasn't died; rather, he cut ties with me in order to honor the wishes of his wife, and to straighten out the misperception others had of what honestly was a lifelong friendship overtaken by grief and neediness. However, much like grief, I hope that misperceptions do not last forever. And in the end, I believe that love and friendship always win.

I left this chapter in because I want people who are grieving to know that your story isn't all the way written yet. MY story isn't all the way written yet. I want those who are grieving to know that grief can steal a part of your heart. Grief can cause you to do things that seem out of character. Grief can cause you to hold on too tight. In a very short time, grief can leave you confused and wondering how things could get so very messed up, even those things that were really good things in your life. Grief can take your whole life and flip it on its head and make it unrecognizable even to you. But here's what matters: Grief can't wreck you if you don't let it. And it can't steal the unconditional love you have for others. Or the love they have for you.

If you have your very own Samuel in your life, hold on to him or her. Love that person unconditionally, but don't hold them so tightly that you crush them. Talk to the people closest to your Samuel to help them understand that the grip grief has on you will not last forever, nor will you be the needy friend forever. If your Samuel has a primary relationship of his or her own, make sure Samuel is clear with the significant other. Make sure your Samuel is grounded enough in his or her primary relationship to be able to say, "I love my partner first. I love my friend second. It's not the same at all. One does not take the place of the other."

I am the luckiest girl in the world because I had people surrounding me who refused to let grief wreck me. Even at my worst train wreck, they loved me with grace I didn't deserve. The absolutely ridiculous and horrific parts of my personality that grief magnified a thousand times didn't scare them away. Even against the threat of losing his own marriage, my Samuel stood by me with that calm voice and said, "It's going to be okay." And he hung on to me as long as he could. For me, as long as he could was at least long enough for me to figure some things out on my own and to get the professional help I desperately needed. I am going to be okay.

And some of that is thanks to my Samuel. No matter how this story ends, I will be forever grateful for his lifelong friendship, his wisdom, his willingness to be a complete dork in order to make me laugh through tears, his ridiculous ability to make me laugh over the phone even while he's picking up his dry cleaning in a variety of southern accents, his ability to keep my secrets and to keep me alive during the hardest time in my life, his stupid dimples, and his unconditional love for me. Maybe not exactly in that order.

DO OVER:
Just because you cannot fix grief or make it stop on your time schedule, doesn't mean you shouldn't continue loving your friends, no matter what anyone else thinks. Grieving or not, be yourself. The people who love you will find their way back through the storm. Love is forever.

Grief almost destroyed me. In many of my stages of grief
(if I wasn't already married) my friends would have had
more luck having a hot romance with:

All of the Power Rangers, Simultaneously
Pirates With Eye Patches
Kris Kringle
Barney the Dinosaur
99 Year Old Gentlemen
Taxidermied Squirrels
Marrionnettes
All of Gryffindor
Joe Pesci   **Hobbits**
Circus People
Unicorns
Lex Luthor
Ebola Monkeys
99 Year Old Ladies
People in Mascot Costumes
The Green Hornet
Jaleel White
Narwahls
Centaurs Trekkies
Drag Queens
Teletubbies
Medusa
Black Widow Spiders
Sparkly Vampires

CHAPTER THIRTY-TWO

BURIAL BINGO

If and when you decide to visit your loved one's grave or burial site, read this.

My friends have loved ones buried on a hillside in a quaint town somewhere, in a plot with no more than four graves. This kind of picturesque cemetery next to a small hillside church is often depicted in beautiful paintings and magazines. This is not my story or my dad's story. Dad was cremated. His ashes are buried in our family plot which has been around at least fifty years, just waiting for more people to fill it I guess. I don't know what this particular cemetery looked like fifty years ago. I don't know if it was a much smaller cemetery that just kept getting exponentially bigger, but that's my guess. The one good thing about where Dad is buried is that there is a huge tree near his grave as some semblance of a landmark, if you can figure out the alphabet soup of latitude and longitude on the map provided by the cemetery.

About a year ago, I finally got up the courage to go to his grave. Translation: I finally got out of my pink sweatpants long enough to go to the cemetery. My youngest three children, then fifteen, seventeen, and nineteen years old, went with me. We stopped by the cemetery office to get a map. My son wondered out loud why I couldn't remember where my own dad was buried. After all, I *was* present for his graveside service. In my own defense, I can only say that in addition to being directionally challenged since birth, I use fast food restaurants as landmarks to get around. It isn't the least bit uncommon for my husband to give me directions that go something like, "You go past two McDonald's and take a right, then past the first Burger King and veer left at Wendy's." And, although this cemetery is certainly big enough to have a drive-through fast food joint in the middle of it, it doesn't. As a brilliant marketing plan, I'll bet I'm not the only person on earth that would consider eating six consecutive Big Macs after visiting my loved one's grave.

In any case, I may have attended my dad's graveside service, but I was in no shape at that point to drive myself *anywhere*. And I didn't look around much as we entered the cemetery the day of his burial. I am posting a copy of the *actual* map of the cemetery, so you can see what the nice lady at the cemetery reception desk handed me to help me find Dad. I have only altered the map in as far as taking the cemetery name off to protect the location of my dad's ashes. All resemblances to real life places and people, living or dead, are purely fictional. *Okay, that might be a lie.*

In all seriousness, I could give you the map, the name of the cemetery, and the latitude and longitude and send you with six Eagle Scouts armed with fancy compasses, and I'm relatively certain you still couldn't find my dad's gravesite. The rows are marked with small brass plates on the ground, with letters and numbers in a graphing pattern. Each section has its own name, like Oak and Maple. The day we visited, we searched about forty-five minutes simply trying to locate the section Dad's gravesite was in. Once we were relatively certain we were in the Maple section (we were wrong), I spent another hour with my three teenagers running the length of the letters and numbers and yelling things like, "H-12...is he near H-12?" "B7? How many steps on the map does it look like B7 is to where Grandpa is?" It was the weirdest combination of Bingo mixed with Battleship and Wizard's Chess that I'll ever be part of. I'm sure wherever my dad is, he enjoyed the length of that exercise because he knew what a terribly patient individual I am. Again, I might be lying. But only about the patience part.

It turns out that the entire grieving process also happens to be the time when I'm most easily frustrated in life. So I am actually proud that we at least attempted to find my dad's grave on our own. I'm also pleasantly surprised that it took me a whole hour and forty-five minutes to have a meltdown; that might not seem like progress, but it definitely was. I think most people who know me would have bet on fifteen minutes tops before the weeping and gnashing of my teeth began.

We eventually gave up, drove back to the cemetery office, and one of their workers jumped in a golf cart and led us to Dad's grave. As it turns out, we were on the complete opposite side of the cemetery, thanks to my less than stellar directional skills. On the bright side, we would have only had to walk about three more miles to find him on our own. It took three teenagers, one lost and grief-stricken soccer mom and eventually a random guy in a golf cart to locate my dad. I don't know how I was supposed to feel when I finally got there. I guess no one can tell you how to feel, but I just felt so very sad. And empty. Christianity runs pretty strong through my veins, so I don't believe my dad's soul is still there in that cemetery. But I guess some part of me thought that by the time I was strong enough to go back there, I would have felt some sort of peace. And I really didn't. That peace never came; just a feeling of overwhelming sadness. I know I will go back to the cemetery again, and I will still be hoping for peace. Or closure. Or a smidgen of understanding as to why everything surrounding Dad's death happened the way it did. For today, however, I'm just aggravated that I wasn't smart enough to bring one of those devices that beeps when you clap like you've lost your car keys, so I could use it to find his gravesite again. My youngest son suggested a forty-foot pole with the Scottish flag on the end to use as a landmark, or a convenient McDonald's drive-thru in the middle of the cemetery.

DO OVER:

Ask for directions in the cemetery office right when you get there, so a cemetery employee can escort you to the graveside. Or bring a picnic lunch, let your children run loose in the cemetery and try to enjoy the chaos that has taken hold of your life.

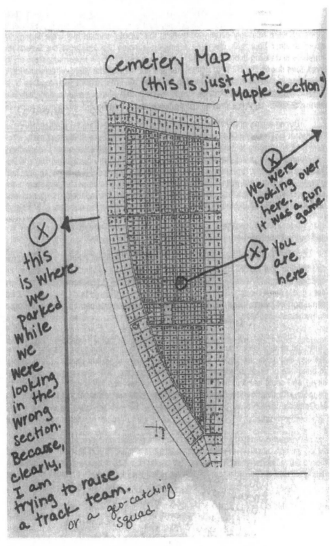

CHAPTER THIRTY-THREE

PROFESSIONAL HELP

If and when you're wondering whether professional help is necessary, read this.

Every day for almost three years, I asked my husband, my siblings, and my friends if they thought I had become crazy. I certainly know that many of the things I did while grieving were in no way normal, at least not for me. I began to seriously doubt my own judgment as to whether I could be trusted to "call myself out" if I had officially turned a corner for the worse. I did not know if my "new normal" could be considered within acceptable societal norms, or if my "new normal" was something that other people were becoming increasingly concerned about.

I will tell you this: The crying had stopped. Almost completely. Maybe not because it should have, but because I was dedicating large parts of my day trying to avoid anything at all – any person, place or thing - that might trigger crying. I had decided not to cry, no matter what. That lasted the better part of a month. But then I stopped feeling well. For the first few days, I thought maybe I was just a little under the weather. I was kind of achy all over and my chest really hurt. And then I went from having occasional chest pains to a constant pain in my chest that hurt so badly I could barely breathe. I couldn't move my left arm at all. My husband took me to the doctor and they did an EKG to make sure I wasn't having a massive heart attack. The irony here is not lost on me, by the way. The doctor came in to tell us that my heart was fine. Good news, there was nothing wrong with my heart.

And then my doctor said, "Well, your heart is fine. But you're obviously not fine, so tell me about your life."

I cried a puddle of tears that day. I was, quite obviously, not fine. The stress had caused the muscles in and around my chest to seize up, cutting off the circulation to my left arm.

And so began the discussion about antidepressants. The doctor said he would start me on an antidepressant, and we'd wait to see if it helped. He explained that it's not an exact science, and each drug reacts differently for each person.

That was the first day of the rest of my life. That was the first day that I was able to admit that I couldn't handle all of the grieving and the stress on my own. Please know that if you are currently on, or have ever been on antidepressants, I have only the utmost respect for the fact that you have taken steps to do something to make your grief and your life more manageable.

But for me, having someone tell me that I probably needed antidepressants felt like personal failure. Maybe even one of the biggest personal failures of my entire life. Not being able to fight off grief, not being able to sleep, not being able to just will away the crying and the sadness, not being able to be happy-go-lucky like I had always been, not just snapping back into shape and getting with the program. I considered all of that a personal failure.

I wanted to solve and fix my grief on my own. I wanted to will it away. That's when I still thought grief could be solved or fixed. Like a math problem. Or a broken piece of furniture. Just slap some hot glue or duct tape on it, and it will be fine.

Agreeing to take the antidepressants and start counseling felt like admitting defeat. I know there are people who do consider that a moment of defeat. But, perhaps luckily, I was in such bad shape that day that I would have done almost anything to not feel so terrible anymore. I thought giving in to a pharmaceutical solution made me a weakling. If I was strong, certainly I would have been able to fix this on my own, right? Plenty of other people live through grief without the benefit of pharmaceuticals, and they can get out of bed, sleep at night, and don't have embarrassing episodes of crying that seem to be completely out of their control, right?

So what was wrong with me? Why couldn't I be one of them?

Grief has given me about seven million moments of coulda, shoulda, and woulda moments of second guessing my entire human existence. The second guessing is enough to make any sane person stark-raving mad. What I have learned is that I can only go forward from here.

And I will go forward without my dad's physical presence in my life. That statement doesn't get any easier, no matter how many years pass and no matter how many times I review the reality.

But I am in command of my choices. I can continue to love my dad, remember him fondly, and use as many of his parenting quotes as I can in an effort to drive my own children insane, or I can sit in a puddle of tears, never get out of my sweatpants and be a ringer for that one parent in every bad after-school special whose children say, "Shhhhh....Mother is sleeping." You know the one I'm talking about...the mother is usually insane beyond words and the teenagers are raising themselves.

My youngest son and I have had more than one conversation about the antidepressant I'm now taking. He, like everyone else, knows I didn't want to take them. But when he asked me, I said, "I don't want to take them, but I also want your memories of your mother to be that person who got out of bed, did her job, loved you, helped you with your homework, and wasn't crying all the time."

I had a moment or two where I wanted to also add, "I don't want your memories of your mother to be of me lying on the couch, eating Nutella from a jar (most likely only with my fingers), and bellowing comments at episodes of Bridezilla or Jerry Springer.

I chose life. My life. I chose to take my life back. I chose to take away any power grief held over me. I chose the life of a pretty good parent, wife, sister, aunt, friend, and youth director that I'd been before April 3, 2012. I liked that girl. She was okay. She wasn't everything to everyone, but she meant something to a group of people who really matter. I chose to use whatever means necessary to feel like myself again.

I accepted the antidepressant and counseling. It took me four rounds of pharmaceuticals to find a combination that worked for me. I hate to call them drugs, a term which I generally reserve for heroin and cocaine. Feel free to read the short notes on grief that are related to antidepressants throughout this book if you'd like more *fun* details of that process. And by fun, I mean ridiculous and sometimes horrifying. Here's what I've learned the hard way: Don't do grief alone. Don't try to shoulder the stuff that's killing you on the inside by building a rock-hard exterior shell around yourself. Grief can break that exterior shell if you don't get the help you need. If you need help, don't stand around and wait for it to come to you. And don't be embarrassed by needing to ask for it. Trust me when I say you're not the only person who has ever needed professional help to get through grief.

Grief really *is* like a bully that beats you up and steals your lunch money. It hurts you and it steals your joy. But you can stand up to it. You can stand up for yourself and say, "No more!"

For me, it took antidepressants and counseling to begin the process of saying, "No more!" I was wrong about the medication. Having to take antidepressants didn't make me weak. Refusing to use a resource that's available to help better manage your life, is just stubborn, pigheaded, and dumb.

I still wish I didn't need antidepressants, and I hope I won't need them forever. I want to be healed enough and strong enough to live my life without them. But I am still working on getting my strength back. More importantly, I'm beginning to see the girl I used to know and like, and depend on, when I look in the mirror. And I think that's what really matters. Grief will not win. I will.

DO OVER:

Don't wait to get professional help if you think you need it. Also, don't bother to slap glue or duct tape on grief. There's no adhesive sold at hardware stores that can hold grief in, which is rather unfortunate.

U.S. states I can no longer return to
due to the number of crying episodes I've had there

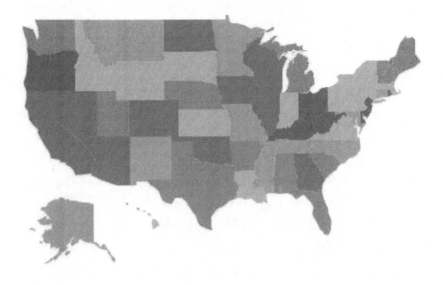

☹ **11** Number of states I have cried in due to grief

👎 **22** Number of opportunities for public humiliation that grief has generated in aforementioned 11 states

✔ **100,000** Reminders to wear sunglasses everywhere I go. And bring tissues.

I will be returning to most of them anyway, but probably in disguise. A girl can only take so much public humiliation while grieving. My apologies to Arkansas, California, Florida, Illinois, Indiana, Iowa, Maryland, Missouri, North Carolina, Tennessee and Texas. I hope NOT to add New Mexico to the list this summer. Update: Afterward I did, in fact, add New Mexico to the list.

CHAPTER THIRTY-FOUR

DUMB CONVERSATIONS ABOUT ANTIDEPRESSANTS

ME: *How do I know if this drug is helping?*

NURSE: *How are you feeling?*

ME: *I don't really know. I don't really feel anything.*

NURSE: *What do you mean when you say "you don't feel anything?"*

ME: *Am I supposed to not care about a single thing? Because, if so, this drug is totally working. I don't care if I go to work.*

NURSE: *Did you go to work?*

ME: *Yes. But who cares?*

NURSE: *Let me talk with the doctor and get back with you.*

ME: *I also don't care about whether or not my kids go to school, or if the dogs are fed, or if anyone eats dinner, or if anyone in this whole house has clean clothes to wear, or if people are mad at me. I don't care about anything. Does that mean this drug is working?*

NURSE: *When is a good time to call you back?*

ME: *Who cares?*

NURSE: *Yes, this might not be the right drug for you.*

This definitely wasn't the right drug for me. Increasingly stupid conversation about antidepressants number two.

ME: *How do I know if this drug is helping?*

NURSE: *How are you feeling?*

ME: *I don't really know. I don't feel worse. I also don't feel better, and I also have no sex drive.*

NURSE: *Like, less sex drive than usual, or none?*

ME: *None.*

NURSE: *None?*

ME: *Yes. None. Zero. Zip. Like an earthworm. Or a nun. Or a eunuch.*

NURSE: *With some of these drugs, your sex drive will come back. Sometimes.*

ME: *So, let me get this straight. My choices are crying all the time, or no sex drive? Because I might decide to go back to crying all the time, under those circumstances.*

NURSE: *When is a good time to call you back?*

ME: *At this rate, my husband is going to leave me for a hot twenty year old. Or possibly an average looking ninety year old. Either one would be better than me right now, because I'm going to end up in a convent. Or living alone with my forty-three cats. Either way, I won't need my sex drive. So just call me back whenever.*

NURSE: *Yes, this probably isn't the right drug for you.*

This also definitely wasn't the right drug for me.

Completely asinine conversation about antidepressants number three.

ME: *In my whole entire life, I have never really thought seriously about killing myself, or spent an entire day thinking about suicide. This is definitely the wrong medicine.*

MY HUBS: *Should I be worried?*

ME: *Can you read me the side effects of this medicine?*

HIM READING TO ME: *May cause drowsiness, nausea, and depression.*

ME: *Does anyone else think it's weird that a drug that's supposed to cure your depression has depression listed as a side effect? What are the other side effects?*

HIM: *Coma and/or death.*

ME: *Oh, terrific. And, furthermore, should you be using a drug that can cause coma or death to cure depression? It seems to me that coma or death might be worse than depression.*

HIM: *Well, I guess at that point your depression is cured.*

ME: *Not funny. I'm stopping this drug. I refuse to put another one of these pills in my mouth. They are making me suicidal.*

HIM: *You're going to stop the drug cold turkey?*

ME: *Would you rather have me continue to contemplate the finer points of my own untimely demise?*

HIM: *No, but are you sure stopping cold turkey is a good idea?*

ME: *I'm doing it. Nothing can be worse than being this suicidal.*

Life is full of cruel irony. If you've ever been through a drug withdrawal, you'll know what I mean when I say going cold turkey off this particular medicine hurt more than at least three of the times I went through childbirth. I was throwing up, had the shakes, my teeth were chattering, and I felt like I had every version of stomach flu I've ever had. All at the very same time. I am not exaggerating in the least. This has not been fictionalized to make it more interesting. By the end of that twelve-hour period, I was no longer suicidal, but I was begging my husband to kill me. As it turns out, this particular drug has been known to cause seizures in many people that go off without tapering down slowly. So, according to my doctor, I was "lucky." I can tell you I felt a whole lot of stuff that day, but lucky *definitely* wasn't one of them.

This also definitely wasn't the right drug for me. Ya think?!

Happily Ever After. On the fourth try, the doctors did finally find something that works for me. I told them that it better not include coma, death, and no sex drive (which is almost as bad as coma or death) as side effects.

If I'm going to have side effects, I want something that would at least make me the subject of some good gossip.

"Remember that girl? You know, the one that always foamed at the mouth?"

"Remember that girl? You know, the one that barked like a dog every time she got too close to peanut butter?"

"Remember that girl? The one who lost her mind and spent a whole day eating pencil shavings?"

If I can't be remembered fondly, is it really too much to ask to be remembered with morbid fascination?

DO OVER:

There is no shame in being on antidepressants. In real life, anything that improves one's quality of life is worth it. But if you HAVE to be on them, at least pray that your side effects are funny enough to warrant a warning label. For example: "May cause intermittent bouts of eating pencil shavings. Please keep pencils away from patient." Or, "May cause ongoing episodes of licking your own arms. Please see your doctor right away if this becomes problematic."

CHAPTER THIRTY-FIVE

FAITH THROUGH GRIEF

If and when you need to read about the progression
of faith through grief, read this.

I do not have a "white light on the mountaintop" conversion story that accompanies my faith. I can't remember a time when I didn't believe in God. God, church, prayer, sacraments, and a faithful life have always been a part of my story. I grew up attending Sunday school, youth group and kid programs, although some of them had less to do with faith and more to do with making crafts that included pipe cleaners, buttons, googly eyes, and lots of glue. At age twenty-four, I became a member of a church staff. Since then, I have been a Director of Youth Ministries at four churches in four states, one small church, two mid-sized, and one large church.

Through this entire grieving process I have tried to remain a faithful, unwavering Christian. I continued to read and study the Bible. I study the scriptures and try to not only make sense of what I'm reading, but also to apply the scriptures to everyday life. I teach the Bible and its life applications to sixth through twelfth graders. I pray. I pray with kids, for kids, during worship, by myself and in groups. I have a relationship with God.

I have heard people use versions of the phrase, a cliché, "If you really believe in God, your faith cannot be shaken." Since my childhood, I have been taught that God should be the center of my life. I have seen people lose loved ones and watched these survivors have some overwhelming senses of peace and gladness that their loved one is with God. And throughout my own grieving process I hoped for some white light moment that would bring everything into focus for me, and would offer faithful peace and comfort. I thought that going through all of the crying, the praying, the bargaining with God, the begging God to make the pain and grief stop, would bring some sort of a revelation that would either point me in some direction, or open my eyes to something God wanted me to see. I thought my faith would be strengthened.

Based on the grief timelines in this book, you know that where I expect to be and where I actually am have often represented two very different locations. And not in what I would consider a good way. For a long time, I was so intensely angry that I refused to speak to God. I had been taught that the God I believe in is big enough to handle little old me. I believe there are things that God allows to happen, but aren't what God *wants* to happen. I know nobody lives forever and that people's bodies give out, and that sometimes we are left without loved ones, without any explanation.

And I know life isn't fair.

But I also believe in miracles. In the Bible, Jesus performs at least thirty-seven miracles that we know about. I studied many of these miracles, and at least two of them involve raising people from the dead. I believe miracles are possible. I don't pretend to understand what makes some people worthy of Lazarus-type miracles, and others not. In fact, I'm not sure one can do anything to prove themselves worthy of a miracle. But on April 3, 2012, I prayed for a miracle. "Please God, save my dad. I will do whatever you ask of me for the rest of my life, if you just let him live." I didn't get my miracle. For whatever reason.

So I have been angry at God. And my faith has been shaken. I had many months of wondering what kind of God would not give a daughter a chance to say goodbye to her father. I spent many months of wondering why my Christianity even matters if, at the end of all things, miracles are only for other people. I spent many months wondering how my life is any different from the lives of those who don't believe in God at all. I have spent my whole life putting God first. And I don't know what exactly comes next in the faith life of someone who, long ago, turned her whole life over to God and, when push came to shove, God seemed silent.

There are some who will give me the "God isn't silent. God was carrying you," or "footprints in the sand" cliché explanation. But the truth is this: My whole body was screaming for help from a God I've always put first. And for at least the past three years, there hasn't been that defining moment when everything makes sense, or when I've found some small measure of faith or peace to be my silver lining.

My silver lining was nowhere to be found on April 3, 2012. Nor in the days or weeks or months that followed.

I originally wrote this chapter near the third anniversary of my father's death. The day he died was wretched. There was no small moment of peace or presence of God that I could feel. It was just wretched. To this day I would consider the experience of dealing with the intense grief over losing someone you love, albeit sometimes funny, mostly wretched. And, at least for me, almost completely lacking in lessons of faith.

I continue to be a person of faith. I continue to believe in God, without believing in clichés like "God's perfect plan," or "God takes people when God needs another angel." And I am still angry at God. There are days when I hope that anger will go away, and there are some days when I don't care if it subsides or not. Even when I'm on the right antidepressant. Sometimes people will disappoint you. In this case, I am disappointed that my dad did not go to the doctor sooner, but I am also disappointed in God. If I believe that God can do anything God wants to do (which is my belief; refer to getting Jonah to Ninevah, the plagues of Egypt, stories of intense healing and resurrection), then God could have saved my dad. But facts are facts. And God didn't.

I continue to be a person who will not give up on faith. But, as always, with tons and tons of unanswered questions and with a faith that can only be described as cracked and in the process of being glued back together. Do I love God? Absolutely. Do I think God's plan is perfect? Absolutely not. My dad isn't here. If this is God's plan, do I agree with it? Absolutely not. I want my dad back.

But, more and more, I believe the strength of one's faith should not be measured by ones' ability to have a steady, stable, unwavering, unquestioning faith for a lifetime, but by one's ability to come back to that faith, even when one is terribly angry at God or torn apart by grief.

"One thing you cannot take away from me is the way I choose to respond."
-Viktor Frankl

CHAPTER THIRTY-SIX

LAST FAITH

Faith For The Long Haul: And Isn't That How Faith Is Supposed To Be?

There are some lessons I needed to learn, and am still learning, about faith. One of them being that there are some questions about God and faith that have no definitive answers. Maybe some of these questions will only make sense in retrospect, and maybe some of them can only be answered by God. For a girl who really, really likes answers and likes things wrapped in a neat little package, faith can be an uphill battle at times. It is almost four years past the day my dad died, but there are days when the raw pain makes it seem like yesterday. And then there are days when it seems like it was an eternity ago since I heard my dad's voice or his laugh. I have spent almost forty-eight months without my dad, and I still don't have the answers that solve my questions about my faith.

I did not initially set out to write a book on faith and grief. I just wanted some answers from God. Or from anyone who would try to answer my questions. I thought, through writing, maybe some or all of this grief might start to make sense. Writing about my faith and my grief was initially for myself. But I decided that if it happened to me, since grief isn't new to humanity, surely there were others who could use my pain and my mistakes as a guidebook for ***what not to do***. Intense grief certainly has had a profound influence on my life, especially on my faith life. I have never, nor will I ever claim to have the perfect faith. I'm not sure if anyone knows what perfect faith is. I do know for sure that I don't know what that looks like. The best I will ever be able to hope for, where faith is concerned, is to be someone whose faith is imperfectly perfect. By that I mean someone who prays, who continues to work at a relationship with God and with other people, who continues to seek the truth through the scriptures, through prayer, and through the faith of other people. As far as my own faith, I think the best I can hope for is to be able to admit that I am an extremely flawed person of faith who tries to get up one time more than I am knocked down. I get knocked down, but get right back up every single time (except for the day I watched all those Bridezilla episodes).

I strongly believe that I will always be someone who loves God and loves others as much as I can, for as long as I can, with everything I have, and with everything I am. I am rather certain I will continue to be someone who always attempts and occasionally succeeds at doing good works, not as a measure of getting my ticket punched into heaven, but because I know there is hurt and struggle and poverty and war and ugly stuff in the world. And because I think that God created me to be someone who wouldn't give up trying, and who always felt that it was worthwhile to use the gifts God gave me to do something that makes one person endure a little less hurt or have a little more hope.

Now faith is the assurance of things hoped for, the conviction of things not seen (Hebrews 11:1).

I don't pretend to know why things happen the way they do, or why bad things happen to people who deserve better. I don't pretend to know how or why tragedy strikes people who are faithful to God just as often as it strikes everyone else. I don't pretend to know what God's perfect plan is; not for my own life and not in general. I don't pretend to know why some people get a chance to say goodbye to their loved ones, and why some people don't. Or why some people have to watch their loved ones suffer, slip away and die, and why other people don't. As far as all of those things are concerned, I'm not sure I'm any further on my faith journey than I was before my dad died. But I know having faith is about believing no matter what, and there are things that are unseen that are still worth believing. And I try to hold onto that faith – seen or unseen - each and every day; even when fury, sadness or desperation fill my life with the grief I'm still trying hard to fight off.

I continue to search the scriptures, and have short moments when I understand how all the pieces of the puzzle fit together. And then, on other days, I search the scriptures and still feel like I am where I was immediately after my father passed away: Trying to make sense of something that will never make any sense at all.

For the last four years people have told me that my faith would get me through. For a really long time, I was not in a good place to hear statements like that. My anger and frustration with a God who doesn't send me answers wrapped in a box with a pretty ribbon on it has been very real. I grew up believing that God answers prayers in three ways: God says yes, God says no, and God says maybe or wait a while. Throughout my journey, I have come to believe God does answer prayers, but maybe there are times when a simple "Yes," "No," or "Wait a while," aren't necessarily enough for someone seeking a more thorough explanation. These last few years, I have had answered prayers, some that have not been answered to my satisfaction, and some that I simply did not want to know or hear the answers to. I grew up with the faith of a largely wide-eyed and innocent little girl. I hadn't yet seen enough of the world to understand that there are some people who claim the world to be simply black and white, chocolate and vanilla, left or right. They are probably the same people who also haven't seen enough of the world to know that it isn't always that simple.

I never ever imagined that life and faith could have so many gray areas. I didn't know you could love a God who allowed so much suffering. I didn't know you could love a God for whom you've also had fury at, and hatred for, when your hoped-for miracle didn't appear. I didn't know you could love a God who left you in a world that is a little less wonderful and a little more empty after the death of someone you love and after the secondary loss of friends or relatives through differences of opinion or seemingly impossible situations. I didn't know.

I thought that with God all things are possible (Matthew 19:26) meant that as long as God was always the center of your life, then somehow, someway, things would always be okay. Not that things would be easy, but that somehow, some way, they would be okay in the end. I never considered that God's version of things working out in the end could look so very, very different than my own version of things working out in the end. This has, perhaps, been one of the more painful revelations of the past four years.

Four years ago, I never imagined for one second that there were moments in life that could turn a somewhat normal, largely rational person into an ugly, hurt-to-the-core, weeping mass that looked for all intents and purposes more like a puddle of messy chaos than a rational human being. I never imagined that the person who weathered the ugliest parts of grief could be so very, very different from the person I saw in the mirror at the beginning of the grief process.

I had always heard stories about God molding people into something different than they were initially. There are many instances in the Bible when God morphed people into someone completely different. I hadn't considered the fact that it would take the worst days of my life, mixed with exhaustion, mixed with whole new lows, mixed with being hurt by some of the people who I thought would always love me and be there for me, to put me on a track taking my life and faith in a very different direction from where I thought I was going.

I have to be completely honest. It has been four years since I lost my dad. There is still no rhyme or reason in losing him, at least not for me. I was caught completely unprepared, completely off-guard, and completely not ready to live in a world without him. It never occurred to me that I would ever have to live in a world without him. I'm pretty sure I've pointed out that I'm probably *not* as forward thinking as you might think. I am someone who loves to gaze at store windows at Christmas and admire the festive packages wrapped in beautiful paper and gorgeous bows. I have always hoped that life would come wrapped in beautiful packages just like those. The realist in me knows that life isn't like that, but it hasn't stopped the idealist in me from hoping that most of life could look like that.

The people who made me the very angriest were those who said early on in my grieving process that my faith would get me through, even though they were probably correct. I am still incredibly sad about so many things that have happened over the past four years, and I am still angry at God. And, in another unmitigated moment of six-year-old first grader faith, I want God to fix me. If Moses can part the red sea, if Jesus can walk on water, if Jairus' daughter can be raised from the dead, if Zaccheus can be invited to dine with Jesus, if five thousand people can be fed with five loaves of bread and two fish, then there is still a part of me that wants God to heal my heart with a giant bandage. There is still a part of me that actually believes that God could, and should, make it happen. If God is taking requests, I'd also like my dad back. And my Samuel back. And, as long as I'm being greedy, I'd like an end to world hunger. And I would like every crematorium in the world to train their employees not to ever tell anyone they have lost someone's body. Even if it's true. And, just in case I am being greedy, because I just might be, I'll take even two out of the four things on that list. Even if I have to wait for forty years in the desert.

When I first lost my dad, all I wanted was for everyone to stop saying dumb things to me, or in front of me, about grief. And about loss. And about God's perfect plan, or God needing an angel, or about this all making sense someday. In four years, my faith plummeted and all but bottomed out. I owe a whole lot of people a whole lot of favors that I can never repay for helping to put humpty dumpty together again. Maybe, just maybe, it takes bottoming out in order to find out who you are and where you are. Maybe it takes almost losing your faith in order to truly find the center of your faith. My faith is still broken and imperfect, but it is a world away from where it was. Over and over again during the past four years, I have gone back to one of my favorite verses in the Bible:

Truly I tell you, if you have faith as small as a mustard seed, you can say to this mountain, "Move from here to there," and it will move. Nothing will be impossible for you (Matthew 17:20).

The first time I held a mustard seed in my hand was in my first year of ministry nearly nineteen years ago. As part of teaching me to be a good youth director, the Christian Education Director asked me to help a team of moms and elementary school teachers to write curriculum, and to teach Sunday school. One of the lessons for that year was on "faith as small as a mustard seed." Never before had I held a mustard seed, nor had I ever seen even a picture of a mustard tree. I didn't know that a seed almost too small to see without a magnifying glass could grow into something so huge. I held onto that seed that first year as a reminder to myself that not only is anything possible with God, but even those with humble beginnings or who felt so small and insignificant and unprepared could, with the right amount of effort, faith, and God's help, turn the world around them into something more amazing than anyone could even dream.

In the last four years, my faith, which I believed had previously grown to be much bigger than a mustard seed, seemed to dwindle into what I considered, at least for a while, "nothingness." During one of my darkest days in grief, I remembered the mustard seed lesson. I took a breath and realized that, even if my faith had dwindled to the size of a mustard seed requiring a magnifying glass to see, it was still there. My anger with God and my sadness and my desperation didn't steal that mustard seed sized faith. It was still present. And it meant that somewhere deep down I still believed in the infinite possibilities of life because of my faith in God. Grief didn't steal my mustard seed faith. Grief doesn't have that power. I had a whole lot of ugly realities to deal with before I could pull myself together enough to work on my faith, and before I could even begin to want to let God back into my thoughts and before I could really pray again without wanting to spit fire or use curse words.

In one moment, my life came crashing down. I lost my dad. I lost my relationship with some of my friends. With my best friend. I lost myself. I was unrecognizable to myself. But eventually some of the ugly wore off. Or at least began to feel less like constantly being stabbed in the heart with daggers. And I was able to go back to my mustard seed faith.

I can't tell you exactly how my faith looks like today. And I can't tell you how yours should look, and when or if your mustard seed faith will return. I can't tell you how long your grief will last, or how to fix it. Although I think I've at least provided you with a pretty solid "what not to do" manual that I hope will help and make you laugh through your own grief. What I can tell you is that I hope and pray that everyone who reads this book, who has experienced or is currently experiencing any kind of intense grief or loss, that somehow, especially on your worst days, you will remember that "mustard seed faith" is always available to you. And someday it will grow to be huge and amazing once again. I hope my story will help you to remember not to quit on yourself, or on your faith. If you aren't that far down the road of grief yet, I can almost guarantee you will, very unfortunately, have days when you will want to quit on yourself, on your faith, and on God. Give yourself some grace. Those days will come and go, hopefully sooner rather than later. If you need to, hold onto this book. I come almost full circle in this book, almost right back to where I started with the phrase "your whole life can change in a moment." Please know that if your own life changes in a moment, there are always faithful people who have been there who will never judge you. And please know that there is always help available.

And perhaps most of all, remember that your mustard seed faith is right around the corner. It might not be today. But eventually, you will turn that corner. And God will be there. Even if you're still angry at God. God will still be there.

DO OVER:
Even in the worst moments, always give yourself grace. Know that you are allowed for your faith to be imperfect. God loves you in whatever form you come to God: angry, upset, joyful, tired, ready to give up, and even grief stricken. And, if you need to, buy yourself a jar of mustard seeds to remind you that even the smallest seed can return to something bigger than any of us can ever imagine. Your faith (or lack of) during hard times does not define you in the eyes of God.

CHAPTER THIRTY-SEVEN

AFTERWARDS

Grief is real. Read this:

It has taken me almost four years to write this book with the hope that someday either Stu or I could hand this book to someone who was struggling through grief, so that they wouldn't have to feel so alone. So they would know they're not crazy. Or that, in comparison, they're not as crazy as I was. And they would know that someone else has been there. In the six months after my dad's death, I desperately searched for a book that was brutally honest about grief and could make me laugh. I never found that book, which is why I felt so called to write this one.

Grief is intensely personal, and every person is entitled to grieve their own way, in their own time. I hope beyond hope that you never experience the level of stress while grieving that prompts your mind to wander separate of your body causing you to wear lingerie in public. Unless public humiliation is something that helps you cope. In that case, have at it! I'll let you borrow my robe. Because of my own moments of public humiliation, I now think very carefully before even considering judging anyone else's life or grief story. The past four years have made me much more capable of listening to the stories of others, without any judgment. Today, at the end of this book, I wish I could be writing a conclusion to grief. I would love to write "And Stuart Rubio lived happily ever after and Heather Wallace lived happily ever after." I cannot speak for Stu, but for four years I have waited for my happily ever after, or a finish line, though I'm not sure there is a finish line for grief. I believe with my whole heart that there is a happily ever after, but it might not look quite like you expect it to. Maybe that's all I've really learned about grief. I will never have closure because I did not get a chance to say goodbye to my dad. On the other hand, he did not suffer. I continue to long for closure that would just close the grief box, one where I could duct tape and nail it shut, and put it on the top shelf in the closet, never to be seen or opened again.

Given the chance, I would like to fix grief or to put it away. But I'm not sure it can be fixed or put away. I think the loss you feel is supposed to linger somewhere inside you. Maybe it's just a matter of learning to carry grief in your own way. Or with the help of prescription drugs.

Maybe the finish line looks less like the triumphant finish line of a marathon and more like folding up a map so you can tuck it away where you might not need it every day, but you can still refer to it when needed. I wish I could be writing today with a pep talk that says "Yes! Four years is the magic number! Snap your fingers and the grief will just go away after four years!" I think everyone knows that life rarely works like that. And I have high hopes that since I'm a little slow on the learning curve, that most of *you* won't need forty-eight months to find a productive way to carry your grief. I began this book with a hopeful promise that Stu and I would make you laugh, at least a little here and there. I hope we have accomplished that much. I also began with a blanket statement assuring you that I am not the expert on grief. I think I have tried to fight the good fight whenever possible. I have cried, I have laughed, I have sobbed, I have behaved badly and then tried to make amends. I have prayed, I have been part of group discussions on grief, I have tried drinking, and I have tried asking God to take this burden from me. And yet, I remain in no way an expert on grief. It took a few scary moments when my body crashed down really hard in order for me to seek professional help.

There is a different way through grief for each person. My hope is that your way through grief is made more tolerable simply by knowing there is someone else out here who is surviving it. Maybe not beating it, but surviving it. And, most of all, that you might know that learning how to carry your grief takes time and often takes help, but you *can* learn how to carry it. You don't have to carry it as a burden. You can learn to carry it as a toolbox or a backpack that gets opened from time to time, when it's needed to help other people.

Grief doesn't have to control or take over your life. Maybe grief doesn't get better. But you don't have to go it alone. And there are survivors around every corner. You can get through it.

Grief does get less awful.

I promise.

GRIEF TIMELINE

20 MONTHS AFTER HIS DEATH

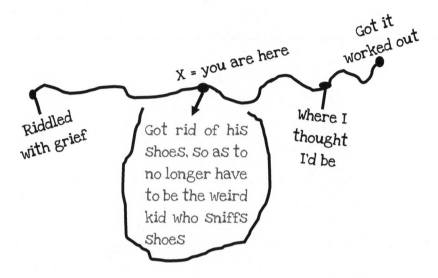

Got it
worked out

X = you are here

Riddled
with grief

Got rid of his
shoes, so as to
no longer have
to be the weird
kid who sniffs
shoes

Where I
thought
I'd be

24 MONTHS AFTER HIS DEATH

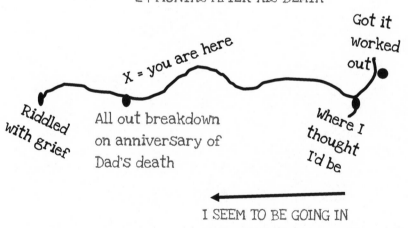

Got it
worked
out!

X = you are here

Riddled
with grief

All out breakdown
on anniversary of
Dad's death

Where I
thought
I'd be

I SEEM TO BE GOING IN
THE WRONG DIRECTION!

GRIEF RESOURCES

In writing a book on grief, it occurred to me that while some of my stories are meant to be funny – and some of them are funny to me...*now* - many parts of grief are not funny. Not at all. Many parts of grief are incredibly painful. In writing a book I could consider a responsible book about grief, I think it's important to include some resources for those who are still really struggling. My good friend Greg Adams is the program coordinator for the Center for Good Mourning and Staff Bereavement Support at Arkansas Children's Hospital. He helped me compile a list of good places to start if you need support:

- If you are having suicidal thoughts or are concerned about a friend or relative who may be at risk for suicide, call **1-800-273-TALK (8255).**

- The Association of Death Education and Counseling (ADEC) offers a service on its website to help you find a mental health professional skilled in bereavement: www.adec.org

- To find a Faith & Grief ministry monthly luncheon or grief retreat near you, visit www.faithandgrief.org or email Heather at Heather@FaithandGrief.org.

- The National Alliance for Grieving Children is good place to start for support for grieving children: childrengrieve.org.

- GriefNet is a very broad website with online grief support and information: www.griefnet.org.

- A very unique website intended for men who may be struggling with depression is www.mantherapy.org. It's very clever and funny, but it also has quality information.

- There is a fairly new website called Modern Loss, www.modernloss.org. It has a more contemporary sensibility than many other resources.

- All of these websites are listed with a brief description on the Good Mourning website, www.goodmourningcenter.org, under Resources.

Resource Suggestions Provided by:
Greg Adams, LCSW, ACSW, FT
Program Coordinator
Center for Good Mourning and Staff Bereavement Support
Arkansas Children's Hospital

FROM HEATHER WALLACE

ACKNOWLEDGMENTS

A debt of thanks, an outpouring of love, and a lifetime of gratitude.

To David: The one man who has loved me for over half of my life, often in spite of myself. Thank you for always being my friend, for being my crazy glue, for making sure our kids got fed, checked their homework, and got them to school especially when grief commandeered my driving and getting out of bed skills. Thank you for always holding my hand, for always being the rock that I can come back to, and for letting me be as crazy as I needed to be in order to find myself. Thanks for always believing in me. I love you.

To Ryan, Gordon, Nate, Hannah & Jack: You are each my heart, my soul, and my reasons for continually getting up in the morning. You make me laugh, you make me think, you each make me better than I am. I am inspired every day by the people you are. I am always so pleased and proud to know each one of you, and to see the wonderful things you are each doing in God's kingdom, in the lives of others, and to be able to call you mine. I couldn't love anyone more.

To Erin, Meghan, Ian, Evan and Sean: I am grateful to have five people who will always understand, with no explanation needed, how I will always feel about Dad, and about losing him. And who will always know how much the phrases "shoo-choo," "the best pizza in the world," and "the last time we'll ever all be together" mean to me. I am so blessed to have all five of you because, as long as I have you, no matter how far apart we are, I know I still have the parts of him that he gave to each one of us. I could never love anyone the way I love you five.

To my mother: You taught me to put myself aside and love other people unwaveringly and fight for them unceasingly if I want them to learn to succeed, even if they don't appreciate it and even if they don't appreciate me. Thank you for being you, and for not actually letting me be raised by wolves.

To Suzi Spiess: You reminded me that even though grief is different for every situation, we can still support someone whose grief is unlike ours. I hope I am able to make you laugh, even with tears in your eyes. I am blessed to know you.

To Johna Hedden: You taught me that even the strongest, most independent women need people to be their friends and to hold them up when they can't do it for themselves. Thank you for always being that for me.

To Amy Logan, The Girl With the Cape: You taught me that believing in myself is the key to life, and reminded me what believing in myself looks like. You have made me laugh harder than I believed I ever could again, and you will eventually be my next door neighbor. I will never see another shiny penny and not think of you.

To Sherry Lira: I know my dad really loved you, more than anything. You were always kind and giving and compassionate to me, especially when I needed it most and, for that, I owe you such a debt of gratitude.

To Stacie Eastman: You taught me that there's nothing (grief included) that KFC and Polar Swirls can't fix, and you've been with me since lingerie, day one.

To Carrie Schuettpelz: You need to find me a ceramic boot at the Christkindl Market.

To Mary Lally: Thank you for taking a chance on a twenty year old who didn't deserve any chances. You used what you knew about corporate business to teach me how to treat people with unmitigated love and compassion.

To Laura Schaffroth: You are an amazing editor, an amazing person, and an amazing friend. I owe you a debt of gratitude that can never be put into words.

To Karen Carver: You taught me how to be a youth director, and how to teach the Bible. You never gave up on a twenty-four year old who was a hot mess.

To Heather Hayes: You have always been my friend, and I will *never again* bake hundreds of cookies with you.

To Dr. Jane Miers: You kept me alive during the worst summer of my life, despite my best efforts to catch every plague of Egypt.

To Ferster (Jennifer Lynn): You have always been my friend for which I am so grateful, and you know what makes Beaners cry.

To the Women of Inspiration Weekend: My forever thanks for your love, trust, kindness, faith in me, and stories of inspiration. I am forever thankful for each and every one of you and the gifts you have brought into my life.

To Dr. Bevan Keating: For not letting antidepressants kill me, and for always bragging about cake. Because of you, I will always trust Canadians, Trekkies and people who match their socks to their shirts. Thank you for understanding my need for perfection, but still being the voice of reason and reassurance when I couldn't be reasonable.

To Amanda Mrozek: Thank you for fighting both for me and *with me* to prove to me that I'm worth it. Thank you for always holding me accountable to myself, and to the person you know I am. Thank you for being my advocate through the pain, and for helping me remember who I was and who I can be. Thank you for fixing me one weekend in Florida in your living room. I'll never forget it.

To Staci Sarkowski: I am blessed to have you as a part of this project, and your beautiful artwork has blessed not only me, but everyone who reads this book.

To Heidi Berta, Sandy Wilson, The Church family, The Zang Family, and Lindsay and Eric Kline: Thank you for helping me through the first part of grief, for always being there for me, and for the ridiculous adventures I've had with all of you and your children.

To Deborah, Derek and Gianna Barger: Thank you for climbing a mountain, and for being our first houseguests. And for finally talking to me.

To my interns David, Christian, Sarah Grace, Maggie and Lauren: Thank you for reminding me what a weird and wonderful job I have, and for keeping me organized and focused, even on days when I struggled to cope.

To the staff and congregation at Second Presbyterian Church: Thank you for loving me, for coming in to visit even if it was for candy, and for never "blessing my heart."

To Julie Staker, David Hayes, Jean Johnson and Scott and Karen Wilson: Thank you for using the "Kohawk connection" to look after our boys while we were far away.

To the Cornish and Passmore Families and In Memory of Grandma Milly: You saved us and put us on the right path, sometimes even the country club!

To Caitlin Camper: You are stronger than you will ever know, and it does get less awful.

To Nancy Coleman: Thank you for gluing me back together, for reassuring me my first summer in Arkansas, and for taking hundreds of my accidental hang up calls from Mo-Ranch.

To Steve Cady: Thank you for holding my hand through some of the worst initial moments of grief and for never letting me fall. Thank you for calling me out, especially when I was most undeniably crazy. Thank you for seven million free lunches at La Mex. Thank you for always letting me make fun of your special, wooden-inlaid boots. Mag put us together. He gave me an enormous gift which I can never repay, in you.

To my youth group kids, past and present, and my youth advisors, past and present, and the "worst youth advisors in the world": Thank you for helping me keep my faith even when times were difficult and my faith wasn't exactly where it should have been. Thank you for making me laugh, usually while I was trying my best to be serious.

In Memory of Rev David P. Laaser: You taught me most of what I need to know about youth ministry with a four square ball, trips to Duvall and at Mr. Pup.

To Matt Malinsky: You recently reminded me why we're still friends. Obviously it's because you're great. And ridiculous. And it's not because you can blame that on my ignorance. If there's ever a movie based on this book, I promise you'll get to play yourself.

To Elias Lutfallah: Thank you for being the one person who knew exactly where I was standing in those first moments of shell-shocked grief. For always saying the right thing. For knowing what the inner struggle looked like and never letting me face it alone. Thank you for being willing to drive a million miles so I wouldn't be alone. May there never be flowers in the lobby of your office. I am only certain of a few things in life. One of them is this: Your mom would be so proud of the friend and of the person you are.

In Memory of Jamie Rubio: I never knew you, but you gave me such a gift through grief. I never believed that grief could give gifts but, when you least expect it, God throws you a life preserver. Thank you, Jamie, for being present on a day when I wanted to quit on life and for somehow engineering it so I was seated next to the weirdo who is your brother. I like to believe that – wherever you are – you and my dad are probably hanging out together.

To Stu Rubio: Thanks for still allowing your child to come to youth group even after seeing my personal brand of crazy. Thanks for making me laugh, often at the most inappropriate times. Thanks for improving my vocabulary, as, well, as, my, understanding, of, how, to, correctly, use, commas. Thanks for making croissants bearable. Prepare for (at least) a year of angry once a month Faith & Grief phone calls. Thanks for making grief a little less lonely and a little more hilarious. And – most of all, thanks for being an unexpected light in one of the darkest times of my life. I could never do anything to deserve a friend like you – so – all credit to God for sending the most unlikely person God could find that would help me find my faith.

To Karen Akin: Thank you for your generous spirit, for bringing Faith & Grief into my life, and for offering the kind of pastoral care that I never deserved, and will never be able to repay.

To Linda LeBron: Thank you for sharing your story which gave me the courage to write about the most wretched parts of my own.

To Fran Shelton, Sharon Balch and Wendy Fenn: Thank you for seeing something in me that I couldn't necessarily see in myself, and for giving me an opportunity to do something for others through trusting me to be a part of the Faith & Grief ministry.

To Ian Waters: "You have been my friend," replied Charlotte. "That in itself is a tremendous thing." - E.B. White, Charlotte's Web I couldn't have said it better myself. You will always be eighty percent better than you think you are. I know that God puts a few miracles on every person's path. Sometimes miracles come packaged with frizzy hair, cardigan sweaters, and other things that are certainly "more than six sigma." Thanks for refusing to give up on me when I'd given up on myself, for making me laugh until I almost drove off the road – repeatedly - and for helping me remember both who I am and the promises I have made. From this day forward, I will never forget that. You are one of the best people I'll ever know.

To my friends who have lost loved ones since I started this project: This is for you. For all of you. You always have someone to call if you feel like grief has taken over your life, and who will listen and never judge. And is happy to drink tea, cry with you, hold your hand, bring margaritas, lift you up on the internet, or whatever you need to make your grief a little less ridiculous than mine. I am happy to be the person who calls you at 4 a.m. to make sure there's no joyriding in your underwear, the person who brings you a lasagna, or the person who drives over to your house to change the channel on your television if the television is stuck on a Bridezilla marathon, or something even worse. Know you are never alone.

GRIEF TIMELINE

36 MONTHS AFTER HIS DEATH

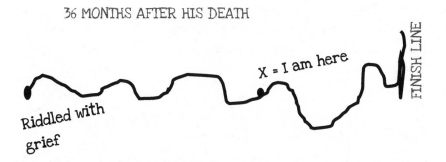

- No longer crying very often.
- Can talk about him without crying.
- Can do things that remind me of him with fondness & not just sadness in my heart.
- Still living a little better due to medicine & counseling.
- Still no closure, but learning to live with it.
- Have not yet been condemned to the life of "the crazy lady who lives alone with her 34 cats. So....progress, right?

FROM STUART RUBIO

ACKNOWLEDGMENTS

To Megan: You are the strength that holds our family together through all of these crazy adventures. I know you felt helpless when Jamie died, because you're a fixer and this couldn't be fixed. Instead, you helped fix me by just being there with a shoulder to cry on and the right words to keep me going one day at a time. Just another example of how we make an awesome team!

To Ashton, Ethan, Evan: I love each of you guys for your unique skills, interests, and the challenges you have and will overcome. It breaks my heart that you will never know your Uncle Jamie the way I did. Always know he loved you very much and is an example of the way you should live your lives. I'd love to tell you stories of his kind heart anytime you're willing to listen.

To my dad and Cheri: You have felt the pain that every parent hopes they never have to feel. I am truly amazed with the strength you've shown in guiding our family through this tragedy. May this book be one of the innumerable ways in which we carry Jamie's spirit forward.

To David: Thank you for the laughs among the tears. You astonish me with your ability to relate to people and support those in need. You most definitely share Jamie's kind heart and have wisdom well beyond your years. I admire your courage and willingness to step out and follow your dreams. But seriously, "I could go for some tacos."

To Grandma Rubio (Mi abuela): The strength and courage with which you've lived your life serves as an example to all of us that call you mom, grandma, and great-grandma (or bisabuela). Thank you for holding my hand through Jamie's funeral and for making me talk about things I didn't want to talk about, but needed to.

To Mom and Dad: Thank you for allowing me to show my weaknesses when the world demanded I be strong. You listened to my stories, cried with me, and prayed with me. You were always a source of strength that I could depend on in a time of great need.

To Adam and Josh: Thank you for supporting me, each in your own way. Whether it was talking to me, listening to me, making me laugh, or sharing your own struggles with me. All of those things brought us closer together. You are both truly an inspiration to me.

To Mark and Cathy: Thank you for your continuous love and support. Thank you, especially, for dropping everything and being there to help all of us get through such a challenging time after Jamie's death. You continue to show us, through your actions, what it means to be loving and caring parents.

To Heather: Thank you for becoming such a great friend *right at the point when I had to move away!* I will welcome your monthly rants from the tables of grief or any other time you need to let out a little bit of your weirdness. Thank you for all of your kind words; you always seemed to know exactly what I was going through and what I needed along this painful journey of grief.

To Karen Akin: Thank you for always being there with a warm embrace, a loving smile, and the natural ability to simply listen. Bringing Faith & Grief to Second Presbyterian has done more good than you will ever know. Not just for me and Heather, but for countless others who need a community to turn to when they are at their weakest.

To Jarrett McLaughlin: Thank you so much for reaching out to me at a time when I was the most in need, but didn't have a church home to surround me. You're calls and messages helped me to restart my life after Jamie's death. "I felt my heart begin to mend into its new shape."

To all of Jamie's great friends: You knew Jamie much better than I did in the last few years of his life. Some of you made the mistake of joining our family football games and left with torn up clothing. Some of you made the mistake of taking me and Jamie on in beer pong during one of my infrequent visits to Lincoln. And some of you I didn't know at all. But I thank *all* of you for being a friend to my little brother.

Things I wish I had known about grieving in advance.

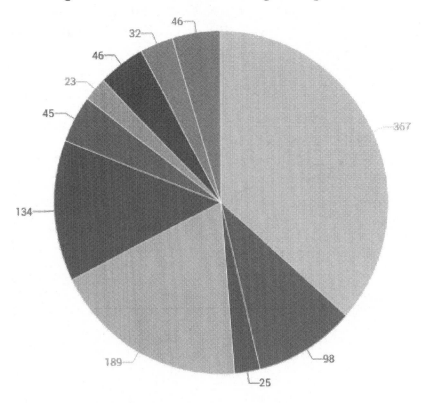

- You'll Never Be Prepared When Someone You Love Dies
- Death Isn't Like On Tv Or In Movies
- Not Taking The Time To Grieve Won't Stop The Grieving
- Talking About Death and Grief Are Awkward For People
- If You're Grieving, Take Any Help That Is Offered
- Grief Lasts However Long It Lasts
- Bring Grievers Gift Certificates For Food
- There Are No "Right Words" When Someone Is Grieving
- You WILL Remember Who WAS There For You When Your Loved Ones Dies
- You Will ALSO Remember Who WASN'T There For You

HEATHER WALLACE

Heather Wallace, The self-proclaimed "Princess of Chocolate Pudding," is a wife and mother of five who is amazingly talented when it comes to vacuum cleaner races, cutting bulletin board letters, pouring coffee, and trying to make sure her house does not become overrun by unmatched socks. Her brutally honest, humorous approach to dealing with grief and her ability to share the story of her journey through the loss of her
father is refreshing, hilarious, if only slightly terrifying.

Heather has been in youth ministry for eighteen years and is currently the Director of Youth Ministry at Second Presbyterian Church in Little Rock. She is both a speaker and Community Educator at Faith & Grief events. She serves on the Annual Events Committee of the Association of Presbyterian Church Educators. Heather is the co-author of Grief Diaries: Loss of a Parent. A native of the suburbs of Chicago, she attended Coe College in Cedar Rapids, Iowa and currently resides in Arkansas with her husband, five children, and one neurotic hound dog.

heather@faithandgrief.org * www.pass the chocolate pudding.com

A great soul serves everyone all the time. A great soul never dies. It brings us together again and again.

-MAYA ANGELOU

ABOUT THE AUTHOR

STUART RUBIO

Stuart Rubio is originally from Omaha, Nebraska, but spent the majority of his childhood in Bensalem, Pennsylvania, a suburb of Philadelphia. He attended the United States Air Force Academy in Colorado Springs and his Air Force career spans almost eighteen years. Stu and his wife Megan (also an Air Force Academy graduate) have three awesome boys and a faithful old dog, Blitz, and the Rubios have been stationed in six different states, as well as in Germany. They are currently assigned to Keesler Air Force Base in Biloxi, Mississippi where Stu serves as commander of the 815th Airlift Squadron, a C-130J combat airlift unit.

Stu can usually be found cheering on the Huskers, Air Force Falcons, any Philadelphia team, and all of the numerous teams his boys have been on. He is also a successful age group triathlete, and is just slightly less weird than his friend, Heather.

reybio10@gmail.com * www.passthechocolatepudding.com

A ministry of compassion and connection.
To host a Faith & Grief event in your area, contact
Heather@faithandgrief.org
www.FaithAndGrief.org

Published by AlyBlue Media
www.AlyBlueMedia.com

Made in the USA
Charleston, SC
01 May 2016